If Ever

Your Country

Needs You

Christine R. Swager

SOUTHERN HERITAGE PRESS
P.O. BOX 10937
ST. PETERSBURG, FLORIDA 33733
800-743-7713

Cover and book design by Byron L. Kennedy III

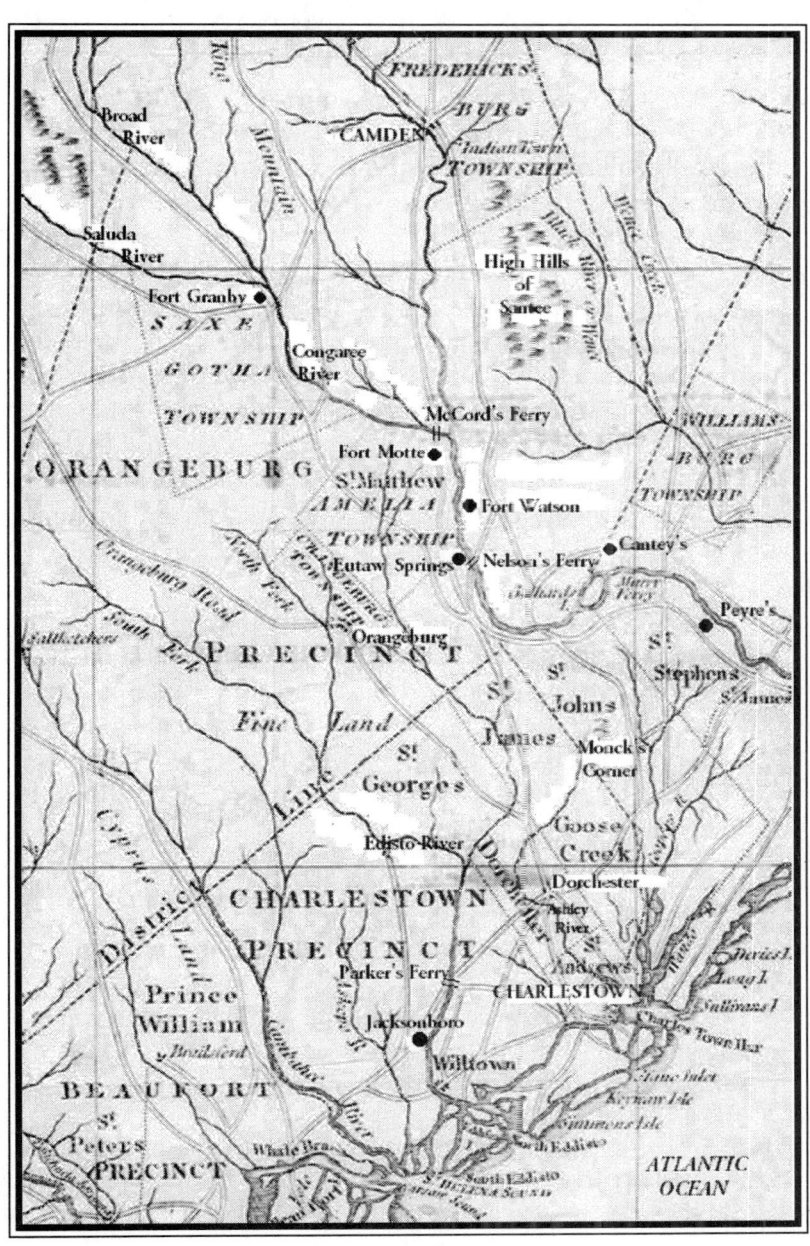

Central South Carolina in 1770's

ACKNOWLEDGMENTS

I am indebted to many scholars, historians and history buffs who have shared their knowledge about the colonial period and the Revolutionary War with me and who have answered my many questions. I appreciate their generosity.

Reenactors, such as the members of the 2nd South Carolina Regiment, provide encampments, living history events, and battle reenactments which acquaint spectators with the colonial and Revolutionary period. Their contributions to my understanding of life in the period are greatly appreciated.

John Robertson, compiler of the *Global Gazetteer of the Revolutionary War* (jr@jrshelby.com), graciously located and mapped sites of Marion's campaign in South Carolina.

I am indebted to my publisher, Byron Kennedy III, whose own interest in the Southern Campaign of the Revolutionary War made *Black Crows and White Cockades* and this book possible.

This story is dedicated to all readers, young and old, who appreciate the sacrifices made for us by the citizen soldiers of the Revolution.

Christine R. Swager

One

Camden, South Carolina
May, 1781

The day was hot, the air heavy with smoke from the burning ramparts about the stockaded village. Mills were ablaze and some of the log cabins smouldered fitfully. What had been, before the war, a peaceful village was now in ruin. The British army, which had occupied the village for ten months, had now retreated and left a wasteland in its wake.

Camden had been a British headquarters for the time it was occupied. Lord Cornwallis, the commander of Britain's Southern Campaign, had waged his operation of terror and control from this little town. Now the British had evacuated the area.

The Battle of Hobkirk Hill, a few days before, had been a British victory, but it had been a costly one. The Continental army had retreated, but not far. They were still a short distance north of Camden, and had been a threat if the British Lord Rawdon had shown any signs of weakness.

American guerilla forces commanded by the Swamp Fox, Francis Marion, were south of Camden. They controlled the roads from Charleston and were not allowing any provisions through to the British in Camden.

The British garrison in the town had been short of food, ammunition and salt. The field hospital had been full of wounded and dying. There had been little hope of relief. Lord Rawdon, who commanded the post, had decided to evacuate the town and head for Charleston. It was that or starve.

The British left burning anything which could benefit the remaining occupants or the Continental Army which would now hold this territory for the Americans.

The British columns had disappeared down the road towards Charleston. They were accompanied by local Tories, Americans who were loyal to the King, their slaves and some prisoners.

It must have been a dispirited group, Jamie thought, those troops who had last year occupied all of the state. The British had planned to sweep north through the Carolinas to a victory in Virginia and, ultimately, in all of the colonies.

It had not been as easy as the British had hoped, Jamie thought. He smiled as he remembered his own efforts to thwart the British plans.

Jamie McCaskill leaned in the saddle and peered into the smoke. His dark eyes reflected his sorrow as he viewed the wanton destruction. He'd seen much brutality, yet still the plight of the local inhabitants troubled him. Would the British and their Tory friends lay waste to the entire land before they were forced to leave? Jamie would do his best to prevent that.

He turned to his companion.

"Ann, I know this troubles you deeply, but it can be rebuilt. With the British gone there will be few interruptions. There will come a time when all is peaceful again and you can move back to Camden."

"No, Jamie. We are not coming back to Camden. Uncle Jack wants us to continue to live at his farm. When Papa returns from the war we will all live there. Although Uncle Jack does well with only one arm, it will be a comfort to him to have Papa and the rest of us helping."

Jamie looked at the young girl who rode beside him. Her fiery red hair peeked out around the edge of her bonnet, framing a face of delicate beauty. Her eyes were blue as the Carolina sky and her skin was fair with a few faint freckles across her nose. She was a wee thing, but it would be an error to mistake her slight build as weakness.

While Camden was occupied by the British, Ann had visited her Tory friend, Rebecca Ryder, and watched the soldiers and noted their insignia. She counted the troops as best she could. She listened to the girls of the town as they gossiped about the comings and goings of the soldiers.

That information had been relayed to Jamie. As a scout for Francis Marion, he knew the value of the information Ann had passed on. He also knew the danger to her and her family if she had been discovered. Conviction, or even suspicion, of spying would mean death by hanging or worse. Yes, this tiny girl who rode beside him had displayed great courage.

The white ribbon cockade he had today placed on her bonnet was to tell the world that this young girl was a true patriot. She was a friend to the partisan leader, Francis Marion - the Swamp Fox. Since few men in the brigade wore uniforms, it was difficult to tell friend from foe in the rough terrain where they rode and fought. Marion had ordered his men to wear a white ribbon cockade on their hats. Now Ann Bixby wore a bright new cockade on her bonnet.

Ann Bixby was very dear to Jamie. When this war was over he intended to return and make his intentions known. However, there was much to be done before he could think of his own future. And Ann's.

Boots, Ann's horse, whinnied and shook his head, troubled by the acrid smell of smoke. Ann quieted him with a firm hand.

"Even Boots senses the unrest here," Jamie remarked. "It is a sad place, this former home of yours. Will you miss it, Ann?"

3

"No. Uncle Jack's farm is home now. Too much happened here for me to ever be happy in Camden. Most of the friends and neighbors we had here were Tory and supported the British. Nothing is the same."

She thought of her best friend, Rebecca Ryder, who, with her family, had left with the departing British. Tory throughout the entire years of conflict, Mr. Ryder had served the British as blacksmith. He accompanied troopers to keep the British and Tory horses and wagons serviceable. Those who actively served the British had left Camden fearing retribution from their former neighbors. There were others whose British support was not so open and many of them were still in Camden. It would not be easy to separate friend from foe in the near future.

Jamie kneed his horse to a slow walk. He sat a horse with grace and the horse and rider moved as one. Since joining Marion's brigade as a scout he'd spent most of the last year in the saddle. He moved about the river systems and swamps with the ease of long familiarity. He was not easy in the cleared area of Camden village, preferring the security of wooded terrain. His horse, Whiskey, sensed his uneasiness and quickened the pace.

As a partisan Jamie rode without uniform but his clothing was distinctive. He wore a linen shirt, leather doublet and leggings. His boots were finely made but had not lately seen a blackening brush. On his head he wore a plaid tam which sported a white cockade, the mark of Marion's Brigade. He was armed with a long rifle and a pistol, and a knife sheathed at the top of his boot. A powder horn and ammunition pouch hung from his neck. A wooden canteen hung from his belt. A blanket was rolled behind his saddle. Everything he needed to live and to fight he carried in saddle bags, and haversack.

"Ann! Jamie!" A voice called.

Ann and Jamie waved at the riders below and rode down the slope where three horsemen waited. All wore white cockades which identified them as partisans and two bore the

4

bright red hair of the Bixby clan. Brothers, to be sure.

Ann smiled at her Uncle Jack. Jack Bixby was attired in articles of the uniform of the South Carolina 2nd Regiment of the Continental Line. That unit had been part of the Continental Army which had been captured at Charleston when the British overran the defenders and occupied the city. As souvenirs of that battle, a scar crossed Jack Bixby's forehead and the left sleeve of his jacket was empty. Jack Bixby was the older of the brothers and a fierce patriot. He and his niece, Ann, had managed to keep the partisans informed of the British strength in Camden during the occupation.

Tom Bixby was younger and heavily bearded. He wore the leather helmet of the 2nd Regiment with its silver crescent. "LIBERTY OR DEATH" was inscribed there. He had fought at Charleston but had not been there when the battle ended. He had accompanied an injured Francis Marion away from the British siege and had escaped capture.

For the last year he had operated under Marion's command, living in the swamps and leaving its safety only to battle with the British. The uniform he had worn proudly had disintegrated in the swamp and he now wore the rough clothing of a woodsman. However, his bearing, as well as an insignia, marked him as a leader of the patriot fighters. He carried the musket, bayonet and cartridge box which had been issued to him in the 2nd Regiment. In addition he carried a small sword, pistol and knife. Behind his saddle was his blanket roll, and from his belt hung his canteen. Haversack and leather pouches hung on his person. He, too, carried everything he needed to survive the campaign on his horse or on his body. He smiled as Jamie and Ann approached and held out his hand to his daughter as she moved her horse close to his.

The third was a giant of a man on a huge dark stallion. He was Black and dressed in leather and armed as Jamie. His face was hardly visible under the large black slouch hat pulled low over his eyes. He, too, wore a white cockade.

5

Ben was a slave on the McCaskill plantation and had served Jamie's father before his death at the hands of the Tory neighbors. Now he served Jamie and rode with Marion's Brigade as a scout. As Ann joined the group he nodded to her and smiled.

"Any sign of the Continentals?" an impatient Jamie inquired.

"None yet," Jack Bixby replied. "Guess they are in no hurry now that the British are gone. Perhaps they are not as eager as we are to have their control established."

Ann had mixed feelings. She was eager to have the detachment of the Continental Army arrive and take control of the town for the Americans. It was important that all the citizens know that Jack Bixby had been a spy for Francis Marion and not a British supporter. But after the formalities, she and Uncle Jack would return to the farm.

Ann's father, Tom Bixby, Jamie and Ben would head south from Camden to join their leader, Francis Marion. They would then harass the British as they withdrew towards Charleston. It was a dangerous business.

The riders moved into the smouldering village. Only a few of the cabins were ablaze but the smoke from the redoubts and mills hung heavy over the town. Men were shoveling the sandy soil onto the hot coals and ashes to contain the damage. Some looked at the Bixby men with suspicion and distrust.

Tom Bixby had been, before the war, a resident of this town but no one rushed to acknowledge him. Recent events had fostered a climate of distrust. Who was friend and who was foe?

When, finally, a contingent of Continentals rode into the village, Tom and Jack Bixby rode forward to meet them. As an officer in Marion's Brigade, it was Tom's duty to report what he knew of the events.

Ann looked at the faded and worn uniforms the Continentals wore. Their blue jackets were threadbare and the beige facings torn and patched. She thought of the white trousers, blackened boots and red jackets which the British soldiers wore as they strutted around Camden. These liberators were not so finely dressed but what a welcome sight they were! Even with evidence of long marches and poor conditions Ann felt she could not have seen a more welcome sight.

Shortly, Tom waved Jamie, Ann and Ben to join them.

"These scouts tailed Rawdon's retreat and can give you more details," Tom explained.

Jamie obliged. "Ben and I watched the columns moving south on what they call the King's Highway, the road to Charleston. They are strung out for miles along the road heading for the High Hills of the Santee. All of the British troops left except for, I understand, a few too seriously wounded to travel."

"Yes," the sergeant of the squad of Continentals replied. "We found about 30 men, many close to death, and a like number of American prisoners to exchange for their wounded."

"They are accompanied by scores of Tories and all their valuables," Jamie continued. "Wagons are loaded with their baggage, and they are accompanied by perhaps 500 slaves. Rawdon stayed till the end and, when he was sure he had taken as many of the valuables as he could carry, he torched the rest."

"Where do you reckon they're headed?"

Jamie did not hesitate. "They'll have to get the Tories and slaves to Charleston, but they'll try to reinforce the British detachment at Fort Motte. There are supplies there that were meant for Camden. They got them that far from Charleston but couldn't get any farther. We took Fort Watson so they couldn't get on this side of the river. We've been watching the ferries and, with the wet spring, the rivers are too high to ford. I expect that Rawdon will try to get to those supplies."

7

"Have any idea what route Lord Rawdon will take?"

"The British surely cannot cross the river at McCord's Ferry since it's too close to Fort Motte. Lord Rawdon won't risk getting troops caught in the river. Marion and Lee have invested the fort and are settled down to a siege. Just a few of Marion's sharpshooters could shoot British soldiers like birds on a fence row if they caught them in the river.

"Marion will have taken all the boats nearby to the west of the river so Rawdon has no choice but to take the longer route. I suspect Rawdon will go to Nelson's Ferry where he has Hessian troops guarding that ferry. It would be the safest place for him to cross. Fort Watson has fallen to Marion and Lee and will be of no use to the British."

"We hear that Marion is a shrewd old fox," commented the sergeant. "I 'spect we can leave Rawdon to him and Lee for the moment. General Greene will be here directly to examine the situation. He's most concerned with care for the wounded as we are far from our last hospital."

"There is a hospital here," Ann volunteered, "but I don't know its condition."

"Pretty bad, Miss," the Continental replied. "Very sad."

An officer in Continental uniform joined the group and addressed Jamie. "You're the scout for Francis Marion?"

"Yes sir, I'm that, along with Ben here."

"We're beholden to you for the information concerning Camden. The figures we got about the strength of the fort here were both accurate and useful."

"I merely passed on the information. Miss Bixby and her uncle, Jack Bixby, gave us the information about the units and their numbers."

The officer turned to Jack. "How did you manage, Sir? Were not the British suspicious of a veteran of the Battle of Charleston?"

"I was considered to be so badly wounded, and subject to fits, that no one paid me any mind. But I stayed at the farm and did not journey to Camden. Ann here, came to

Camden and visited Tory friends with meat and vegetables and returned with the information we passed on to Jamie and Ben," Jack explained.

The officer turned to Ann. "And no one suspected?"

"No Sir," Ann replied. "Before Uncle Jack returned to the farm from Charleston, I lived here. After we moved to the farm I came with my aunt when she brought goods to trade. We brought food to the Ryders, who are Tory, and were our neighbors when we lived in a cabin here in Camden. I wore my old clothes and was dressed like the children of the village so the British paid me no mind. I tagged after my Tory friend, Rebecca Ryder, and the other girls. They were all excited about the soldiers and talked of the comings and goings of the soldiers. They always talked of Lt. Col. Tarleton, whom they thought handsome, and of Lord Rawdon, whom they thought ugly. I didn't ask any questions and they thought me disinterested because I was so young. I noted the insignia and tried to estimate the number in the units I saw."

"And no one noticed?"

"No, Sir. I just tagged along. Many times the girls would talk of who was here, and where they were going, and when they would be leaving. Other times I just watched, especially for Col. Watson who was always after General Marion. His unit wore those light uniforms so I could always tell when the Buffs were in Camden. And Mrs. Ryder helped care for the British wounded and sick so she often mentioned how many were sick with swamp fever. She says Lord Rawdon suffers greatly from its recurrence."

"Many of the British who have lived in the north find this weather damnable," the officer agreed. "It's said that Lord Cornwallis moved on to Virginia, rather than return to South Carolina, because of the toll the heat and disease took on his troops."

"I know not why he went north," Tom Bixby spoke. "I'm glad he is gone with that brute, Tarleton. No one was safe from that savage and I fretted constantly about the safety of my family. Especially Ann, who took such risks on our behalf."

The officer nodded solemnly. "What are your intentions now, Cap't Bixby?"

"Now that you are in control of the town and my brother is established as a loyal Whig and no Tory, we'll leave to join Marion at Fort Motte. He'll want to know of the evacuation of Camden. Rawdon has made a tactical retreat as the British would starve if they stayed here. We were letting no supplies through from Charleston and your army was pressing from the north. Their salt supply was gone and food and medicine scarce. No, Rawdon is not beaten. He retreated to prepare to fight again and Marion and Lee need to be ready."

"How will you travel? The road to Charleston is clogged with the British."

"Yes, so we'll cross the Wateree and go down the west bank while Rawdon is on the east bank. We will probably travel as far as possible before crossing the Congaree as the Orangeburg area is heavily Tory. We need no ferry as these horses have spent many a mile in the water. We can swim the Congaree close to the bluff at Fort Motte with no problem. Besides, it might be a nice break from the heat. It's getting to be a scorcher!"

Business finished, Tom turned to Ann. "My Wee Ann, stay close to the farm till things are settled here in Camden. There's no need for you to visit here any time soon. Times are still dangerous."

"Yes, Papa," she replied and moved her horse close to his as he reached for her. After a quick embrace he turned to Jack.

"I leave the most precious things of my life in your care, brother."

"I'll watch out for them, Tom," Jack promised. "Have no fear for their safety. Just watch for your own."

Jamie reached for Ann's hand and squeezed it. "Stay safe,

Ann. And pray that we'll meet again soon."

She nodded and turned her horse away and followed Uncle Jack up the slope toward the Kershaw house which stood on a rise overlooking the town. There they turned and waved one last good-bye. Then they kneed their horses to a faster pace.

"It's too hot to tarry here," Jack decided and he pushed forward toward the farm.

It was late afternoon when they arrived home. The large house at the edge of the bluff over the swamp stood as a sentinel against the green wilderness beyond. The house was large and designed for a large family which Jack and his wife, Rachel, had planned. But that was not to be and Rachel had borne and buried four children. Now the house sheltered Jack's brother's family: Ann Bixby, her mother Ellen, or Nell as she was called, and Ann's little brother, Tad. Here they had weathered the last terrible year of conflict. What would the next year bring?

Fort Motte

It was late when the three riders approached the bluff where Fort Motte stood. It overlooked the spot where the Wateree and Congaree Rivers join to form the Santee. They had found the journey difficult due to the terrain, and had occasionally altered their route to avoid meeting Continental patrols.

General Greene had sent scouts to travel the west bank of the Wateree to keep watch on Rawdon's movements on the east bank. Although the Continental Army and Marion were all fighting for the same cause, Tom wanted no confrontation with them in case there was any misunderstanding about loyalties. Locals, both Tories who supported England and Whigs who supported the Americans, knew that the white cockades signified that the rider rode with Marion's Brigade. The soldiers of the Continental Army might not be so well informed and Tom didn't want to spend any time explaining.

From the shore across the river from the fort they could see campfires spread out over the area along the bluff and beyond. The siege had been underway for some time so there was no need for the siegers to skulk in the darkness. As Jamie and Tom waited on the shore, Ben scouted the area for difficulties.

On his return he reported, "Seems like Lee's horsemen on the bluff and Marion down yonder toward the fort."

"Then we move a little south of the fort and cross at Col. Thomson's. His land slopes to the river and we can come up to Marion's lines from there."

Decision made, they moved farther downstream, then walked the horses into the swollen river. In a short time they were on solid ground again, and waited patiently for the sound of any pickets who might be guarding the area. Marion would not have overlooked this crossing.

Hearing the faint sound of movement on the hill above, Ben raised hands to his mouth and started the series of bird calls which would identify them as Marion's men. They had no desire to be taken for hostile intruders. After a pause the calls were answered and the three riders moved forward.

Once recognized by the pickets they moved up the mile or so towards the fort. Mrs. Motte's plantation house had been fortified by the British because it stood on the bluff commanding a view of the entire area.

Seeing Marion's position, Tom hurried to report to his commander.

"I'm glad to see you, Tom," Marion greeted him. "What has happened in Camden?"

"The Continentals are in control of the town as Lord Rawdon has withdrawn."

"I'd heard talk but didn't believe it. Last night the British in the fort started cheering on seeing campfires across the flood plains in the High Hills. From their hollerin' it was plain they believed them to be Rawdon's troops."

"That they are and accompanied by the most obnoxious Tories and their baggage. The wagon train and marchers stretch for miles. Seems they took about 500 slaves with them."

"Have any trouble?"

13

"No. Some Continentals are on the west of the Wateree keeping track of Rawdon but we avoided those patrols. Wanted to waste no time getting here."

"I 'spect Rawdon could cross at Nelson's Ferry and be here in about 48 hours," Marion thought aloud. "The only way to dislodge the British here before Rawdon can reinforce them is to burn the house. A few burning arrows on the roof should do the trick."

"A shame. It's a fine house and a shame to destroy it," Tom commented. "Another casualty of war."

Marion nodded. "Col. Lee has talked with the lady and she has agreed. Even given us a bow and arrows to do the deed."

Tom knew that Marion would have been reluctant to talk with the lady. He was a quiet man and not particularly known for social graces.

However, Col. Lee and his Lee's Legion had been sent by General Greene to assist Marion in the attempt to dislodge the British from their many small posts around the state. Lee, of a fine Virginia family, was polished and comfortable in such company as Mrs. Motte's.

Marion spoke again. "And your family, Tom. Are they well?"

"Yes. A Whig posse rode to Jack's place thinking him a Tory since his family had sent food to their Tory friends in Camden. Intended on hanging him, as they had hanged scores of Tories in the area. I assured them that Jack was part of your intelligence network and they hesitated. Then Jamie and Ben arrived and that convinced the riders that they had no quarrel with the Bixbys.

"Then we accompanied Jack and Ann to Camden to meet with the Continentals so Jack is established as a loyal patriot. I suspect they are safe for now. The only danger is Tory militia but few are in the Camden area now that the British are gone. The Whigs have hanged about 500 of the British supporters in the last few weeks."

Francis Marion shook his head sadly. "What great guilt we

all share for this misery. I pray this will soon be ended. I know it comforts you to know that your family is safe. Let us pray that soon all of the families of the brigade are safe."

Tom took his leave and moved over to the militia lines on the slope of the hill overlooking the fort. The plantation home was strongly fortified by a stockade, and a ditch. An abatis, a fence of sharpened branches pointing outwards, surrounded the position to deter any enemy from storming it.

Behind Marion's militia lines was an artillery piece, a six-pounder, resting on a mound of dirt.

"How many do you suppose are defending?" he asked no one in particular, as he surveyed the situation.

"About one hundred and fifty, both British regulars and Hessians we're told," was the reply. "Also some local Tories. Perhaps two hundred and fifty in all. Won't be easy to get them out even with the fire from the six-pounder."

"Where did that come from? We had no artillery when I last rode with you."

"General Greene sent it."

Tom moved about the line and then moved off to find more familiar faces in the brigade, men he'd ridden with this last year. From them he heard disturbing news that General Marion had sent in a resignation and asked leave to go to Philadelphia. Philadelphia? What would the Swamp Fox do there? Tom wondered. He'd have liked to ask Marion himself but the general was a moody person and not given to confidences. Someone must have tweaked his tail good to have prompted a threat of resignation. Perhaps the morning would bring some explanation.

The morning was bright and sunny. The siegers went about their business as if nothing important was happening. Behind the lines, out of view of the British garrison, preparations were being made to use the tactic which Marion had learned fighting Indians. They were preparing balls of resin and brimstone which would be stuck to the ends of the arrows, lighted, and then shot on the roof. The shingles were tinder dry from the last few hot days and would burn easily. The men who prepared the arrows were men who had had homes burned out when Col. Wemyss had torched every Whig farm in the low country. They relished their assignment.

Waiting till noon when the morning dew had dried from the shingles, a last ultimatum was delivered to the defenders. When the offer was scorned, the attack began.

"Once the roof is afire, shoot anyone who tries to extinguish it," Marion ordered his sharpshooters.

Jamie and Ben took their places, out of range of any British musketry.

Tom Bixby stood close by the men as they poured powder into the barrel, then rammed the patched shot, tamping it tightly in place. They replaced their ramming rods, then added powder to the pan and waited.

"Take the men on the left, Jamie. You fire to the right, Ben. A few knocked off the roof ought to drive the message home."

"Yessir."

When flaming arrows struck the roof setting shingles afire, British soldiers appeared on the roof trying to tear off the flaming shingles. A round of grapeshot from the six-pounder raked the roof and impeded the effort.

Jamie took his aim, and fired. He hit his man, and the impact knocked the soldier off the roof. Ben and the other riflemen were clearing the roof of the firefighters.

Seeing it was useless to persist, the British commander hung out a white flag of surrender and the fire was quickly extinguished.

Since the command was divided, Lee took in hand the regular British troops while Marion accepted the surrender of the Tories.

That evening Mrs. Motte entertained all the officers with provisions which had been secured at the fort intended for Camden.

Tom was enjoying the festivities when Jamie came to him with an urgent message. Tom relayed it to Marion who left the company and rushed, sword in hand, to a place where troopers were hanging prisoners.

Seeing the unfortunate Tory hanging by his neck, Marion shouted, "Cut him down, damn you. Cut him down."

Ben rushed to lift the unfortunate man up to release the strain of his weight on the rope. "He ain't dead," Ben announced and Jamie cut the rope and the limp man fell to the ground.

"What are you doing?" Marion demanded of Lee's troopers. "What in God's name possessed you? And by whose authority?"

The usually quiet little man was in a raging temper.

"Just hanging a few prisoners," a trooper replied.

"By whose authority?"

"Colonel Lee."

"I'm in command here. For every prisoner you hang Rawdon will hang more of our good men. Who will we exchange for the men they hold?"

The troopers in their fine green jackets stood tall beside the feisty little militia general in his ragged red jacket and scorched helmet. Like David among Goliaths, Jamie thought. But Marion, who disliked any brutality and was especially rigorous in his regard for the treatment of prisoners, was not through. He gave explicit orders to cease this activity which were reluctantly obeyed. Leaving Tom and Jamie to record the names of the troopers involved in this escapade, Marion left.

Duty done, Jamie accompanied Tom back toward the brigade's camp.

"A nasty business," Tom remarked. "A nasty business. Never thought Lee's troops would engage in such activity."

Jamie nodded in agreement. "In our other operations with them, like at Fort Watson, I never saw any sign of such brutality."

"I 'spect the Good Book is right. The devil will find works for idle hands. As long as they campaign they fight like soldiers. When idle, they forget discipline."

Suddenly Jamie ventured to ask. "Is it true that Marion has threatened to resign his commission and leave?"

"That's what I heard."

"Seems Lee and Sumter told Greene that Marion took horses for other than military use and could send many to the Continental army. Greene wants to mount a cavalry."

"We don't have horses to spare without dismounting our brigade," Tom observed. "Marion will never agree to that. Where did you get your information about the horses?"

"Ben. He hears many things and usually his information is reliable."

"Let us hope he is wrong about this. I've no stomach to fight for anyone other than Marion."

"Nor me," Jamie agreed.

The Commanding General of the Southern Continental Army, Nathanael Greene, rode into Fort Motte to meet with Lee and Marion.

There was great excitement among the victors of the engagement. Most of the brigade had not seen a uniformed Continental in a year, other than Lee's Legion who had accompanied them in campaigning in the swamps. Now it was a reality. The Continental Army was here in South Carolina and they'd heard about this general and knew he intended to stay.

Jamie was asked to accompany Marion to record the meeting and prepare to write reports and correspondence. With less scouting required, Marion had decided that Jamie's education would be well used as his aide. Although literate, Marion did not relish writing reports and letters. He had kept his communications to a minimum when, in the swamp, paper was rarely available. Now Greene would want periodic reports and Jamie was Marion's choice to provide them.

Jamie watched as the two men met for the first time. He

was struck with the differences. Greene was still a young man in his late thirties while Marion was approaching fifty years. Greene was tall and heavy while Marion was very short and wiry. Greene's face would be considered by many as handsome while the hook-nosed Marion bordered on being ugly. Greene's complexion was fair, almost florid, while Marion's skin was swarthy and leathery.

But there were some similarities. Greene moved with a decided limp on a stiff knee. Marion's gait was awkward on his malformed ankles and knees. Greene's Continental uniform of blue jacket with beige facings was dusty and worn. Marion's red jacket was patched and his helmet was scorched. The lines of fatigue and great cares marked both faces as they met.

After the initial greetings, Greene spoke. "I hope my letter regarding the horses has reached you and the matter resolved. I had no intention of dismounting your brigade as I know the swiftness of your strikes depends on fast mounts."

Marion seemed mollified, Jamie thought.

"It is difficult to keep the militia engaged," Marion complained. "They are required to provide service for 60 days and some have more than doubled that, but their circumstances are dire. Their families have need of them and many are without ammunition, food or pay. How can I sustain a fighting force with so little?"

Greene hesitated. "Your state is invaded and much will be required to rid the territory of the British. Our country needs us. We must continue the task and now is not the time to let the efforts flag. I have not had one day of leave and have left my family in distress and shall continue to the end."

Jamie admired the speech but recalled that things were different in the north where Greene had served. Each year the armies had established winter quarters and fighting virtually ceased. General Washington and his staff officers had their wives and families with them while the war waited. He'd heard that Mrs. Greene was always among the women who accompanied Mrs. Washington and her husband. General Greene may not have had leave, but he'd fathered four children during the war!

Jamie had heard that even now Mrs. Greene was being escorted to Camden where she would visit with the Kershaw family. The Continental soldiers he had talked with told of the fancy clothes she wore, military in style. A beautiful lady, the general's wife was, they said.

In South Carolina there had been no respite. No snow or ice had impeded the British and Tories and every day was perilous. Marion had no wife but he'd also had no headquarters. His office was a fallen log in the swamp and his bed was a pile of pine straw covered with a scorched blanket. Surely Greene had pledged his career to his army but Marion constantly risked his very life. Only vigilance and cunning had kept him alive. 'Tho every man of the brigade knew of the sacrifices, it seemed that Greene did not fully comprehend them.

Greene continued and enumerated the recent gains of the brigade. "You have rendered Fort Watson and Fort Motte useless to the British. Your brigade has succeeded in the destruction of Fort Balfour on the Pocotaligo and routed the Tories at Four Hole Swamp. You've done great service with the militia you command. We must not fail now."

Marion's face was stoic, Jamie noted. Would the praise be sufficient to make the little guerilla fighter rethink a resignation? What would become of the effort without Marion he wondered.

Greene outlined his strategy. With Camden evacuated, other British outposts would be attacked at the same time. With all under attack the British could not provide large numbers of reenforcements to any one garrison.

Marion nodded in agreement a relieved Jamie noted. The Swamp Fox seemed eager to continue the struggle.

Meeting over, Lee departed towards Fort Granby about

thirty miles to the west, a British stronghold in the midst of Tory territory. Sumter, they understood, had captured the small garrison at Orangeburg. And the old Indian fighter, Andrew Pickens, was raiding British and Tory positions in the western part of the state.

Marion was to operate east of the Santee River, dogging Rawdon's withdrawal. They had to be sure that the British commander did not turn and double back to attack Greene. And there were Tories in the area to be humbled. And, if occasion arose, Georgetown would be attacked.

Marion assembled his militia, whistled his command and led his men across the Santee. The men were in high spirits. The former grumbling had ceased. The men with the white cockades were back in the saddle. Marion was on the move.

Three

The Garden at Bixby's Farm

The rain had finally stopped and the new day was sunny and warm. Ann, dressed in her work clothes, stopped to slip wooden clogs on her feet, and to tie a large straw hat on her head. She then headed to the kitchen garden.

It had been a wet spring and all indications suggested that would continue, so work was done when weather permitted. The gardens close to the house were growing well but needed tending. The rain that had made the vegetables grow so well had also nourished a large crop of weeds.

Ann loved the garden. It was lush and green and flourishing. When Uncle Jack and Aunt Rachel moved down the Great Wagon Road from Virginia, they had stopped over to rest in the Moravian community of Bethabara farther north. They greatly admired the gardens those peaceful and pious people designed and tended. Uncle Jack organized his garden in that fashion and it was a place of beauty as well as utility.

Uncle Jack himself had paced out the plots which were squares separated by wide pathways. The seeds were planted in diagonal rows from corner to corner through the squares and the pattern was pleasing to Ann as she worked.

In the fields farther from the house, the slaves cared for large plantings of sweet potatoes, corn, beans, squash and pumpkins. There were rows of carrots and beets and other vegetables which had to be grown in great quantities for the household.

Sugar cane was grown for the household's use since blocks of island sugar were not available. Sorghum and molasses were adequate substitutes and the cane also provided the means of making rum. And there was a small stand of tobacco for Uncle Jack's pipe. Slaves also tended the cash crops and the plantings of hay and grain for the horses and other stock.

Since trade had almost halted after the British blockaded ports, Uncle Jack had grown only a few crops for trade and extended the food gardens. It was the abundance of food which had allowed his wife, Rachel, (Ann's "Aunt Raye"), and Ann to journey to Camden to trade food for what was available. On these trips they had carried food to their old friends, the Ryders, now Tory. This gave Ann an opportunity to visit with Rebecca and to listen to the girls of the village talk of the soldiers. Ann had also watched for insignia and estimated the number of men and horses in the town. This information had been passed on to Jamie, Marion's scout. Jack and Ann met Jamie in the small hammock, or small stand of firm ground, in the swamp below the house.

Ann stood leaning on her hoe as she thought of the last year and wondered where the Ryders would go. They left in the long convoy of wagons with Lord Rawdon, headed for Charleston. What would they do there? She wondered. And had Papa, Jamie and Ben arrived safely at Fort Motte? It would take days for word to get back to Camden even about fighting so close to the Wateree River and Ann was not a patient girl. In fact, the Scots were known for their lack of patience, and this young lass was no different.

"Wait up, Ann," Tad called as he jumped off the porch and ran to her. "Aunt Raye says for me to check for snakes in the garden."

"I haven't seen any," Ann informed her little brother.

"Aunt Raye says that a few might come into the gardens close to the nesting birds to get eggs or baby birds," Tad explained.

He took the hoe from Ann and marched up and down the paths between the planted squares, peering closely between the plantings.

Her little brother looked so like a soldier walking his post that Ann smiled. Tad, almost ten, did not have the red hair of the Bixbys. Nor did he have a single freckle. His hair was dark and wavy, his skin clear and fair. He favored his mother's side of the family and would be a tall and handsome man Ann knew.

Ann, on the other hand, was a Bixby through and through. Her red hair matched that of her father and Uncle Jack but she had only a few freckles. Her mother had insisted that she keep her skin covered from the sun as she burned so easily, so her skin was very fair. While Papa and Uncle Jack were tall, Ann was tiny taking after her Grandmother Bixby who had been very short.

"Nary a one, Ann," Tad announced with satisfaction, returning the hoe to Ann. "Aunt Raye says for me to get the little cart and the young boys and tote over loads of manure from the horse barn. It needs to season some before we apply more to the garden."

Tad hurried off. Ann smiled as she watched him go. He had worried so when he thought his father was dead. Tom Bixby had been reported killed at Charleston where Uncle Jack had been wounded. When Jack had returned home he confided to Ann, her mother and his wife that Tom had not been in Charleston during that shelling. He had left with a few other men who helped take an injured Francis Marion to safety along the Santee. They would carry on a guerrilla war. But, thinking Tad too young to keep the secret, they had withheld that information.

It was just a few days ago that Lord Rawdon was preparing to leave Camden and no longer able to protect civilians. Whigs, who supported independence, were roaming the area in posses hanging Tories who had supported the British. Jack Bixby was a target since no one except a few patriots knew the visits to Tory friends in Camden were a cover for spying. Few knew that Jack Bixby had provided the intelligence to Francis Marion, the Swamp Fox.

Tom Bixby, Jamie and Ben had arrived to thwart any attempt on Jack's life and, when trouble did arise, they were there to provide ample protection. When the riders came in the night it was not Jack Bixby but Tom Bixby who answered their summons and explained the role of the Bixby household to the vigilantes bent on revenge.

Tad had been reunited with his father. Now he knew that Ann had spied for the patriots by visiting the Ryders. If he was saddened by the loss of his friend, Harry Ryder, he never mentioned it.

Now Jack Bixby had been recognized by the Continental Army as a patriot so no more trouble was expected. Of course, renegade bands of Tories could come into the area, but Uncle Jack's household was prepared for even that. They would not let their guard down. And now that Tad was aware of the role of the Bixby household in the struggle, he participated with great enthusiasm. And, no longer thinking himself a fatherless child, he was again happy.

Tad, actually named Thomas for his father, was a changed child since the secret was out. Ann smiled as she watched Tad saunter off toward the horse barns. He had been Aunt Raye's shadow during the past year. It had been necessary to keep him away from the swamp where Jamie met Ann and Uncle Jack. So Tad rode daily with his aunt to oversee the workers and had grown to love the farm.

Ann turned again to her task. The kitchen garden and the gardens close to the slave cabins were the responsibility of the women. The oldest slave, Hattie, supervised the herb garden, but Ann spent much of her time tending the larger kitchen garden. Although all who lived on the farm enjoyed the bounty of fresh vegetables, there were a few grown under Ann's care for the family alone. Today she would harvest the last of the asparagus and English peas which were for Uncle Jack's table. The asparagus roots had yielded most of the edible shoots for the season but a few remained for Uncle Jack's dinner. The rest of the ferns would be left to nourish next year's crop.

Now the heat would soon wilt the English pea vines which clung to the branches pushed in beside the rows to support the vines. Ann carefully pulled the ripened pods and placed them in her woven basket.

The few days that Papa and Jamie had stayed at the farm they had enjoyed the peas. Ann knew that they ate sparingly in the swamps. They lived on sweet potatoes roasted in the ash of the fire, boiled rice and a little wild game roasted on a spit over the fire. However, when pursued, there was little time to cook or eat. And fresh vegetables were rarely available.

Many farmers had been burned out and several killed by the British or their Tory sympathizers. There were many hungry in the state and would eat little until a good crop was available. The excess food raised by the Bixby farm would help ease the suffering.

The Bixbys had concealed much food in the last year. In addition to the root vegetables which had been mulched in the fields, other crops were left in fallow ground, unmarked, in case enemies came to loot. Foodstuffs were hidden in caves in the banks in the bluff overlooking the little stream which ran to the north of the house. A few cows were hidden in the swamp and were milked by the slaves to provide milk and butter for the farm. The best horses were hidden in the swamp and only the mules and work horses were kept when they could be seen.

However, they were lucky. The British dared not move in

small groups around the countryside so their patrols had not ventured toward the farm at the edge of the swamp. The farm was so isolated and so distant from any wagon trail that few visitors approached. However, Jack Bixby had prepared his household for attack. The women had all been taught to use the rifles, and slaves had practiced on fowling pieces and muskets. There had been no shots fired but they had been ready.

Ann hoped that, with the British gone, all would be safe. However, she knew that Tory militia still roamed the state. Reports of atrocities still circulated. Uncle Jack would not let his guard down, Ann knew. She thought of the still present danger as she pulled the pods.

When all the peas had been gathered Ann sat in the little hut in the garden and shelled them. The rattles on stakes had not completely intimated the birds and a few brave ones pecked on ripening strawberries. The blueberries which grew on bushes in a hedge along one side of the garden would soon be turning blue and the birds would relish those if not dissuaded. Perhaps Tad could plan some sort of scarecrow which would frighten the birds.

Rows of carrots needed weeding Ann could see. The kohlrabi and brussel sprouts were more hardy. There was lettuce to pick before it wilted in the hot weather, and garlic and onions growing profusely. Radishes and early spinach were ready for the table, but the peppers, celery and cucumbers would come later. Red cabbages were slow in maturing but Nell Bixby had them grown here. The regular cabbages were grown in the field with the row crops along with parsnips for winter.

Melon vines tangled against the garden fence, split quarter log posts with split rails. The fence was to keep wild animals such as hogs and deer and wild steers out of the garden. There was nothing that could be done about rabbits, Ann thought.

At one end of the garden, a great trellis of stout wood supported grape vines, and close-by, gooseberry bushes were heavy with unripened fruit. Without interruptions, there would be an abundant harvest this year, Ann thought, and was grateful for it.

The herb garden, a great favorite of the rabbits, adjoined the vegetable garden. Nell Bixby, Ann's mother, was a fine cook and she decided what was needed here. It was a beautiful garden of lush plants of every form and color: anise, cress, lavender, dill, sage, yarrow, sweet basil and sweet marjoram, camomile, tansy, citron, and a few others.

In the medicinal garden the herbs were those plants that Hattie insisted on tending: the plantain, wormseed, wormwood, poppies, comfrey, wild camomile and many others. She often wandered in the swamps returning with roots which she planted in shade and watered profusely. Ann never knew the names as Hattie only identified plants by their uses.

"For fever," she'd say or "For the headache."

However those plants, which she reckoned were medicinal, were well cared for and had eased much suffering. Hattie had been with Rachel Bixby's family since birth and had been one of the dower slaves which Rachel's family had given to her and Jack Bixby when they married years ago.

Hattie's two sons, Ezra and Noah, and their families had also come from Virginia with the newly married Jack and Rachel. This slave family was close to the Bixby family and lived and worked near the house. Hattie was the undisputed head of her family. She supervised the house and kitchen work and tended the sick and injured.

Ezra and Noah were able-bodied and willing workers. They supervised the care of horses, rode with Rachel to survey the crops and carried out her orders. They directed the cane pressing, and the charcoal kiln. They organized the hog butchering in the fall, and the planting in the spring. They maintained the buildings and kept things running as Uncle Jack wished. But most important of all, they were loyal. In this time when the British had tried to turn slaves against masters and to work against their owners, Hattie's family had remained

28

loyal.

The other slaves who worked the fields looked to Ezra and Noah for leadership and they had provided it. They had organized the slaves at Jack Bixby's farm into a small army which would defend the house and farm against the enemies. At Rachel Bixby's orders they had posted guards to keep watch against strangers and had planned a defense of the property.

When Jack Bixby returned from the war, he had improved on the defense with weapons and drills.

Hattie approached the garden and looked over the herbs she tended so carefully. She nodded her satisfaction.

"Miz Ann," she scolded, "It be too hot here for you. Best you go inside before you burn. Miss Nell don't want you blistered."

Ann stood, gathering the empty pods in her apron, and moved to the mulch pile just outside the garden fence. Tad and the young slaves were moving wagon loads of fresh manure to a pile close-by. Others were turning the old pile of manure with wooden forks to let the air circulate and the manure ripen so it would be ready to enrich the garden soil. Nothing was wasted on this farm.

Settling on the porch, out of the sun's hot rays, Ann thought of her father and Jamie and wondered where they were now.

Nell Bixby came out on the porch, wiping her hands on her apron.

"Where are they now, Mum?" Ann asked.

"I don't know, Ann," her mother responded. "I only hope they are safe but they are beyond our help. We must trust in God's care. And pray, Ann. Pray."

Ann recalled how many times in the last years her mother had given Ann that same advise. Prayer had sustained them through the darkest days. Surely it would not fail them now.

Four

After Ft. Motte

The brigade was in high spirits. The evacuation of Camden had diminished British control and influence in the area Marion's men called home. Now, with a lesser threat to their families, the militia turned out in greater number. Many assembled at Cantey's Plantation, where Marion often mustered his militia. The Canteys were long-time friends and loyal Whigs. The British withdrawal from Camden made this retreat even safer than before.

"Tom," Marion spoke quietly.

"Sir," Tom replied.

"Have the men and horses ready early in the morning. We'll ride along the Santee and keep an eye on Rawdon."

The men ate hearty that night and packed saddle bags and ammunition pouches. Horses were carefully tended, and the camp settled early. This was not a new procedure but there was a new enthusiasm. With every mile Rawdon moved toward Charleston, Carolina was closer to being free. That was an exhilarating thought for all the men who rode with the Swamp Fox.

Before dawn Marion whistled the signal to mount and move out and the ragged band rode away from Cantey's quietly. Even with the increased excitement the men moved furtively. Only the clop of horses hooves in the soft dirt marked their passing.

Jamie and Ben, scouting ahead, spotted the end of Rawdon's columns.

"Where do you suppose they're headed?" Jamie wondered aloud.

"Hard tellin'" Ben replied. "Seem to be wanderin'. Could be they lost?"

"Don't seem to be moving very fast to cross the Santee. They have to cross at Nelson's Ferry but they don't seem in any hurry."

"Guess so," the taciturn Ben nodded.

Later, Jamie reported to General Marion. "Seems Rawdon split off a column to accompany his baggage. Looks like they're heading to Wadboo. The rest are crossing at Nelson's Ferry."

"Can we take the baggage?" an excited Marion asked.

After numerating the strength of the column accompanying the baggage Marion decided against the attempt. Even such a prize was not worth the risk when he would be so seriously outnumbered.

Marion followed along behind Rawdon's main force but did not attempt to intercede.

"He's blowed up his post at the Ferry," Ben reported.

"Guess he thinks we need it to cross the Santee," Jamie exclaimed. "Of course, the Continentals need that ferry worse than we do, but since Greene is already on the west of the Santee I guess he won't need it now."

With Rawdon across the Santee, and the British baggage out of his reach, Marion traveled to Peyre's Plantation, a new hideout. The plantation was situated as the Bixby farm, on a high ridge surrounded by small streams and oozing swamps. The men fell to building brush arbors and lean-tos. Marion called for militia to fill his ranks. Some refused to come.

"Jamie, keep a list of the men who refuse to come. They will be published as enemies of the state. And arrange for some of the men who have fought in this campaign to visit home to take care of their personal affairs. Will you need to return to your plantation?"

"No, Sir. The last word was my mother has things in order as well as can be expected. With the British pushed farther from the PeeDee, I suspect there will be little Tory activity. Our most serious Tory neighbors have been killed so there is little danger there. I'm needed here, Sir, and I will stay."

"Fine. Inform me of the men who will stay as I need to send patrols out to intimidate the Tories. And I need intelligence from Georgetown so you and Ben must provide that. Those poor people have suffered enough under the British yoke. If we can dislodge the garrison it will be one less haven for those brutes who disregard military customs. Our men who traveled to Georgetown to return the British officers paroled at Fort Motte were brutally treated."

Jamie and Ben were a tired pair when they arrived back at Peyre's from the Georgetown vicinity but they had good news.

"The garrison has about 80 regulars and a few Tory militiamen."

"Then write Greene and beg leave to reduce that place," Marion ordered Jamie. "And indicate the urgency of the matter. The men who went home will return in force when they hear we ride to Georgetown. With that place in our hands the British will have only Charleston as a point of supply."

It was not in Marion's nature to wait when ambition rose, and he moved his men to Cantey's and sent out the call to the militia to muster. Men responded in great numbers until he was almost at full strength when they set out for the coast.

What excitement! Georgetown, at last.

"Tom, deploy the men and start throwing up entrenchments. We have the force and Georgetown will be ours."

The men set to work and stopped only when the light failed. Sleep would not come easy tonight as the troops were filled with anticipation. The prize was within their reach.

Marion intended to teach the British a lesson. But it was not to be. The British slipped out to their vessels under cover of darkness and sailed out of Winyah Bay.

In the morning Marion's men found the garrison deserted, the cannons spiked, rendering them useless.

"Search the town," Marion ordered. "It is rumored that they kept a large cache of arms here."

When the search was over, Tom reported, "If there are arms there we did not find them. However, we confiscated liquor, clothes and a large store of salt."

"Arrange to conceal the salt in safe places around the countryside. Our people have need of it. Then, prepare to leave this place. We will ride to the Santee and move closer to Monck's Corner to see what Rawdon is up to."

But their departure was delayed when the British ships were spotted still skulking around the bar.

"They may be waiting for us to leave so they can return," Tom suggested.

"Probably so," Marion agreed. "Leave a small guard to discourage that, and to level the works."

That done, Marion led the remainder of the brigade across the Santee. Since Greene had not shown any enthusiasm for the Georgetown expedition, Marion ordered his men to round up dragoon horses for Greene's Southern Army. Perhaps that would appease Greene.

It took Jamie a moment to recognize his commander. The old red singed and patched jacket was gone and Marion stood, resplendent, in a new uniform of regimentals. From the plunder he had also acquired two mules to carry his baggage. The singed blanket had been replaced with a new one, but the charred helmet of the 2nd South Carolina Regiment he kept. Now that he fought in concert with the Continental Army it seemed prudent to look more professional.

In the guerrilla campaign appearances had been of little importance, and a singed blanket had provided sufficient cover. Though any man whose blanket was whole would have traded gladly, Marion would not seek his own comfort at the expense of any member of his brigade.

"Tom, I need a messenger with a fast horse to relay intelligence to General Sumter," Marion commanded.

Tom Bixby had seen a rider approach in great haste, speak briefly to Marion, then depart the way he had come.

"The British have landed reinforcements in Charleston. Brought three regiments of foot soldiers numbering about 3000 men from Ireland."

"From Ireland, you say. The June heat will give them a hot reception," Tom commented.

"We must get word to Sumter. However, in case he neglects to share the information with General Greene, we'd best send the word to him independently. Sumter is getting increasingly belligerent."

Tom agreed to that. Sumter had always been prickly but, of late, he'd been outright disagreeable. It would be charitable to blame it on the serious wounds Sumter had suffered at Blackstocks where he'd scored a great victory over the hated Tarleton. In any case, Tom had no desire to ride with any but Marion.

Orders soon arrived from Greene for Marion to muster his militia and join Sumter in preventing Rawdon from moving towards Ninety-Six, a strong star fort to the west of Orangeburg. Greene intended to siege the fort in the prominently Tory area. It could only succeed if Rawdon could be prevented from going to Ninety-Six with reinforcements.

Marion sent out the call but the militia did not muster in great numbers.

"They won't come, Tom," a dispirited Jamie reported. "They know the action is at Ninety-Six and those who march have no intentions of going that distance in this heat. Even

34

some mounted will not respond, arguing that this is Sumter's action and they have no stomach for him. They seem to know when Marion will command and it is only then the militia have any enthusiasm for a fight."

And they did not come. There was not a sufficient number for an engagement so the British under Lord Rawdon hurriedly marched the 200 miles to Ninety-Six in the blistering heat. The siege was broken but it had been costly. Fifty British soldiers from Ireland, still wearing their woollen uniforms, died of sunstroke. Tom had been right. Carolina's summer heat was not kind to the reinforcements from Ireland. But General Greene had been forced to abandoned his plans to take the British fort.

"The Swamp Fox will not like this," Jamie mused as he read the report from General Greene. Greene's displeasure was not veiled. He had written of his failure to capture Ninety-Six since Lord Rawdon had not been prevented from interfering. Now he was ordering Marion to cooperate with Sumter in any manner Sumter chose. No, that would not sit well with Marion.

And would Sumter take advantage of this new directive? Of course he would.

"I feel like I'm glued to this horse," a tired Jamie complained. He and Ben had scouted along the Santee and into the Orangeburg area. Marion had his intelligence but the British declined to engage Greene's army so the brigade was constantly on the move. Jamie wondered if this might be deliberate on Marion's part. If Sumter couldn't find him, there could be no direct orders.

But Sumter's courier did find them and the plan was brilliant. However, it was rather too ambitious and complicated for the troops involved Marion thought. Continentals and militia would have to coordinate their efforts and coordination was not something that combination did very well. However, Lee and his Legion would operate with Marion and that pleased the Swamp Fox.

Jamie had always been amazed at the relationship between Light Horse Harry Lee and Francis Marion. Lee, from a prominent Virginia family, had recruited his own legion and named it, humbly, "Lee's Legion". He had designed and provided his men the striking green jackets and white trousers. With their black boots and tall brass helmets with horsehair plumes they were a handsome unit.

On the other hand, Marion was a farmer, descendent of French Huguenots who fled religious persecution in Europe and settled along the banks of the Santee. He was small and swarthy. He was a quiet man given to moods of silence and remoteness. His guerilla fighters had been ragged backwoodsmen, and even the more affluent militia members would seem plain to the Virginians.

Lee had had the finest education wealth could provide, and his manners were grand. Marion had the education available to a small planter and he was naturally shy and uncomfortable in social settings. But each commanded unwavering loyalty and respect from the men who served under them. Each had a distaste for excessive bloodshed, unless it was the enemies'. Each would withdraw rather than take risks of heavy casualties. And each enjoyed the plotting, the maneuvering, the chase. Yes, Jamie thought, they were unlikely allies but they campaigned well together. Perhaps even Sumter's plan could work with Lee and Marion present.

The plan was to attack Monck's Corner and isolate the British commander, Colonel Coates, from Charleston. Coates commanded part of the Irish troops newly arrived in the country. When Sumter's troops started to move, Coates recognized the danger. He abandoned his position and started to withdraw towards Charleston. He stopped at Biggins Church, a huge brick building with walls three feet thick. The following day he burned much equipment and fired the church, and moved even closer to Charleston.

Lee captured Coates' rear guard and rushed towards

Quinby Bridge, on the route Coates was expected to take. But the British had burned the bridge and Lee's cavalry could not cross the marshy expanse along the creek. Artillery protecting the bridge wounded several of Lee's troopers.

However, the action had panicked many of the British green troops. They fled, then returned when they saw their commander defending himself with a sword. With the situation at a stalemate the action broke off.

Coates retreated again to regroup at Quinby and prepared to face the attack. Would his troops stand or would they break and run?

Time would tell.

It was mid afternoon when Marion's men arrived at Shubrick's Plantation on Quinby Creek. The plantation house was a structure with two stories. The outbuildings, gardens and slave quarters were surrounded by a stout rail fence. The British commander, Col. Coates, had occupied the house and stationed his soldiers in a large hollow square formation in front of the house. A howitzer or small cannon covered the approach to his position.

Jamie accompanied Marion as the Swamp Fox discussed the terrain with Lee. Lee's cavalry had already engaged the British and earlier had driven them to their present position.

"Thought we had them whipped but they got some backbone and regrouped," Lee commented with wry humor. "That unit arrived from Ireland in time to get quick marched to Ninety-Six with Rawdon. The Carolina sun was not kind to those new soldiers in their woollen uniforms. I heard that fifty died on the march of sunstroke. Thought maybe they'd run out of gumption by now."

Marion was quiet as he surveyed the terrain. "We'll take unnecessary casualties if we attack them head on. Sumter will have artillery pieces with him and that will even up the fight. Have any idea of how many men Coates commands?"

"About 500, I would guess, and not a Tory among them.

They are all British trained troops, regulars of the 19th Infantry of Foot. If the odds are right we can take them," Lee stated with assurance.

Marion nodded in agreement and added, "And artillery will give us those odds."

Beyond the range of the British the brigade made ready for a fight. The weapons were clean and equipment checked. The brigade would charge after the artillery fired.

But Sumter arrived in the late afternoon without artillery. "I don't bring field pieces when I chase retreating British," he boasted. "We'll attack now."

Marion and Lee disagreed but, Jamie knew, it was little use. Thomas Sumter was known to be hardheaded and, when in command, would heed no advice. Attack they would, and Jamie knew that none under Lee's and Marion's commands would be too pleased with the plan.

Sumter's men moved to take the slave cabins where they had sufficient cover. A detachment of about 4 dozen men under the command of Col. Taylor was ordered to make a direct attack on the house. Taylor's men reached the fence but were beaten off by a bayonet attack by the British. Seeing Taylor in trouble, taking heavy losses, Marion and Lee advanced across the field to help.

Jamie and Ben moved with the others and gained the fence.

"Stay down and take what cover you can," Marion shouted. "Fire under the rails! Stand only to reload!"

Jamie and Ben were quick to obey. Shooting from a prone position they took their shots carefully since there was no ammunition to waste. However, the rifles needed to be rammed to be reloaded and it was necessary be exposed to the enemy fire. Jamie hoped that those British soldiers were not as accurate as Marion's men.

The sun was low in the sky and Jamie was down to his last few shots. He intended to make them count He stood to ram his shot and, as he was replacing his ramming rod, he heard

Ben yell.

"Jamie! Down, boy!"

Quinby Bridge

"Jamie! Down, boy!"

Jamie dove down in the dusty dirt behind the rail fence, face first, his rifle extended in front of him. To the right front he saw the danger, a musket aimed his way. He moved his rifle to aim at the chest between the green facing on the red uniform jacket but it was too late.

He saw the enemy fire and heard the thud of the bullet hitting flesh but it was not his own flesh. Looking to the side he saw Ben flinch and knew he'd been hit. But Ben didn't falter. He stood firm and fired.

Jamie saw the explosion of blood, bone and tissue as the bullet smashed into the enemy's face. He would be dead before he hit the ground. That soldier would never see Ireland again!

He heard Ben muttering his satisfaction with the shot and knew that, 'tho wounded, Ben was still on his feet.

Jamie saw the enemy's line move back as he heard

Marion's shrill whistle. It was time to withdraw but he had a loaded rifle. He aimed deliberately at the nearest redcoat and squeezed the trigger. The bullet found its mark and a satisfied Jamie turned to Ben just as the huge man's knees buckled and he went down.

Jamie crawled to where Ben had fallen behind the rails of the fence.

"Where you hit, Ben? Can you move?"

"Yessah, I won't stay to die here. I'll get to my hoss."

Ben rolled over and pushed himself up on his knees. Jamie saw Ben's bloody side, above his waist on the left. Grabbing Ben's uninjured side Jamie helped his slave to his feet.

Around him men were moving to retrieve the bodies of the dead and horses were brought up to load the corpses. Someone brought Whiskey and Midnight, Jamie's and Ben's horses, and rushed to help Ben mount.

With his foot in the stirrup, Ben used his right hand to pull himself up and into the saddle. He slumped as the pain gripped him.

Jamie took Ben's rifle and his own, mounted, and led Ben's horse from the battlefield.

Away from the now occasional firing, they paused.

"How far can you ride, Ben?" Jamie asked.

"Far's it takes," Ben answered as he coughed up blood. Wiping his mouth with his sleeve, he reassured Jamie. "Not much broke."

Jamie knew it was not safe to stop to tend to the wounded but he hoped they would not ride long. It was a quiet ride. There would be time for discussion later. Something had gone horribly wrong at the battle and these men knew where the fault lay.

A silent group led the horses of their dead comrades, the men who had given their lives to the cause. Hardly a word was spoken but thoughts were of the dangers. They had carried other dead from other skirmishes, but none as bitter as this.

Lee's troopers were part of the procession. They, too, accompanied their dead. It had been an encounter of less than an hour, but a costly one.

Soon, deep in the swamp, a halt was called and Jamie, with the help of others, got Ben off his horse and to the ground. The surgeon, who rode with them, moved among the wounded. There were many more seriously wounded than Ben. One officer had been wounded five times. He was a large man and, clad in a uniform, had been an obvious target.

Ben commented wryly, "Good I wore buckskin."

Pickets were posted on the trails around the camp although no one expected to be pursued into this awful swamp. Men started preparing a common grave for the dead from Marion's Brigade and the troopers from Lee's Legion.

Fires were started and a meager meal of corn mush was prepared. Jamie washed his down with swallow of water from his canteen, water laced with vinegar to keep it from going sour.

Ben declined food but drank from his canteen.

Finally, when the light was fast fading, the surgeon got to Ben. Jamie lighted fat pine and held the torch close to Ben's side. The surgeon knelt and tore back the leather which the bullet had penetrated. He probed the path of the missile.

"Looks like the bullet hit the lung. Think we can get the slug out," he remarked to Jamie. "And the impact surely broke a rib or two, but they'll heal."

This surgeon rode with Marion on many occasions and he knew the value of this patriot. Everyone who rode with Marion knew Ben. The size and strength of this giant partisan was well known. He'd carried many a wounded man from the scene of battle. Now, they gathered around to offer whatever help they could.

While the surgeon worked at removing the bullet, Jamie held the torch steady. Others held Ben so he would not flinch under the surgeon's probing.

Ben uttered not a sound but his muscles were tense and his skin grey. Jamie could only mutter an occasional encouragement and, thankfully, it was soon over. There was always little time so the surgeon's work was hurried. After the metal was removed, he packed the opening with lint.

"That needs to heal from the inside out so's not to fester. He should be cared for in a safe house, out of this swamp and its poisonous air."

"Can he ride?" Jamie asked.

"If he can stand the pain. If not too much's tore up he should heal fast. But the wound needs tendin' to."

Tom Bixby approached. "Thank God things are no worse than they are, Jamie," Tom exclaimed.

He looked off to the side where men were working at their dismal task. "Too many good men down, but it looks like Ben will make it if we get him someplace where he can be cared for."

"I'll not leave him, Tom. He's too vulnerable if left with a local family, even if we could find one we could trust. Even if the enemy doesn't find him, General Sumter might. He confiscates slaves to give as enlistment bonuses to his men."

"Sumter says he only takes the slaves of the enemy - the Tories."

"Any man who has something Tom Sumter wants is his enemy," Jamie replied with bitterness. "I'll not leave Ben."

"I can ride," a weary Ben insisted. "I can ride."

He looked over where the men were laying the bodies in the freshly dug muck. Every man was thinking of the possibility of being buried in an unmarked grave in a dismal swamp. Ben had no desire to risk such a fate. As long as he had breath in him, he could sit a horse and escape this place.

The swamp was wet from the heavy rains and the fires smoked for lack of dry wood. But the men in the swamp welcomed the smoke as protection against the insects swarming in the sultry night air. And the smoky haze which settled in the swamp masked the odors of the night: the smell of unwashed men who had fought in the blistering heat; the sour odor of rotting vegetation; the musky smell of muck; and the odor of death and fear. All permeated the camp as the men went about the grim task of burying their fallen comrades.

The wounded were moved as close to the smoky fires as safety permitted in an effort to keep the insects at bay.

Later in the night, around the fires, the conversation was bitter with much recrimination. All thought that Sumter should have waited for field pieces. And much indignation was expressed over his protection of his own men and the waste of many good men of other commands. The bodies they had buried were of friends, comrades, patriots. Such a waste! Such a waste! And the blame was laid at Sumter's feet, this man who had let his reputation and daring override his good sense.

Marion, followed by his slave and constant companion, Oscar, approached Tom and Jamie. After inquiring about Ben's condition, the talk was of the battle and the future.

"Most of these men will leave during the night," Marion announced without rancor. "They will get a half a sack of salt as pay for the most horrible two months ever a man endured. They will leave."

Plans were made to move those who would remain to Peyre's Plantation on the bank of the Santee River. The brigade would muster there later but the men were in much need of rest. Some of the men would stay with the brigade.

Certainly many of the Black men would remain. Some, like Ben and Oscar, were slaves of men who rode in the brigade. Others were slaves who had escaped when their owners had been hanged or driven out and the slaves scattered. Some had belonged to Tories. Some had families but had no idea where they could be found. In the meantime, when other men left the brigade to return home, these men had no place to go. They were vulnerable if they left the protection of the brigade. These Black men looked up to Ben and, during the night, stopped to inquire of his condition and to pay their respects.

It was a restless night for Jamie. The air was heavy and sultry. Insects swarmed over men and animals making rest difficult for all. The smoke from the small green wood fires was hardly a deterrent to the blood sucking and biting little beasts. Horses stamped and swished their tails trying to discourage the pests. Men slept fitfully in the sweltering, miasmic, unhealthy air of the summer swamp. And Jamie listened to every sound from Ben who groaned and writhed as he tried to rest.

Jamie knew Ben was not safe yet. Any wound could go sour and result in death. Jamie thought of the men in the shallow, soggy graves and knew that Ben would be spared that. Jamie vowed that if Ben should perish he would not bury him in a swamp but in dry ground in a marked grave.

Jamie's thoughts were shared by many of the men who slid out into the night to depart. Jamie heard them go and knew of their sorrow and their fears. It was a sad time when a man's only prayer was to die in his own bed and be buried in the family graveyard.

Light came early with an eerie mist over the swamp. The air was heavy and unhealthy. There was little food and less time to eat. The men who had not deserted during the night mounted and prepared to move out.

Ben was now rarely coughing blood so it seemed that the bleeding had been stemmed.

Tom Bixby and Jamie helped Ben mount his horse and the three started through the swamp, north away from Charleston and the British who still occupied it.

Miles later, they heard horses behind them, and moved into the heavy green growth beside the trail. They had no time to deal with the enemies now.

45

"If it be Tories, leave me," Ben told Jamie in a hushed voice. "I can hide, and ride towards Camden later. Save yourself."

As they readied their weapons, Tom gave a shrill bird call which was answered with the call of the brigade. A relieved pair rested their weapons and waited.

Francis Marion and Oscar soon joined them

"The men have been informed when they'll muster at Peyre's. The business of the brigade has been attended to. We'll ride with you to Camden," Marion informed them.

"We're aiming to go to Jack Bixby's farm, Sir," Tom Bixby explained. "Ben can be cared for there. I know Jack would be glad of your visit if you would rest a few days with him and his household."

"Thank you. We'll accompany you there but must press on. I've sad news to take to friends whose men we buried in the swamp. Then I'll join the brigade at Peyre's."

Jamie had been privy the evening before when Col. Lee and Marion vented their anger about their casualties. Lee swore never to fight with Sumter again and expressed his intention of informing General Greene in great detail what had gone wrong at Quinby.

Marion added, "I suggest we take the trail into the Black River Swamp. The shade will be welcome and the softer trail will make Ben's ride easier."

Nothing more was said. Nothing needed to be said. That route would avoid the High Hills where General Greene's troops were encamped. The hot summer had drained the troops who were not used to Carolina's blistering heat and high humidity. The High Hills of the Santee offered some relief. Greene's troops were resting but Marion's brigade was weary and battle scarred. Marion wanted no part of Greene's campaign until his own men were refreshed.

Jamie said nothing as they turned toward the Black River and its swamp. It was rumored that only Marion could navigate that swamp, but Jamie knew that the Bixby men were also equal to the task. He knew that the easiest route was preferable. Ben's condition was not good. Jamie prayed that Ben's stamina would suffice.

Six

Bixby Farm

It was a sultry day and, as the late afternoon wore on, the Bixbys sought the shade of the porches. The air was too heavy with humidity to even move in a faint breeze.

Supper was being readied in the outdoor kitchen as Nell had already determined that there would be a cold supper. It was just too hot to eat a big meal.

"What are they doing?" an irritated Jack Bixby demanded. He rose from his seat and leaned on the porch railing. "They know better than to race those horses in this heat."

Ezra and Noah were riding at a furious pace along the bluff to the south of the house.

"And what are they doing there?"

The fields where the slaves had been working were to the west of the house, and the work had been finished an hour or so ago.

The horses approached the house and an excited Ezra raised in the stirrups and shouted, "Riders comin'! Riders comin'!"

"Where?" Jack responsed. "And how many?"

"Half dozen, I reckon. And in McGirt Swamp. Didn't wait till they come out. Come to tell you."

Noah pulled his horse to the bottom of the steps as Jack descended.

"Give me your horse, Noah," Jack demanded. "I'll ride with Ezra to check our visitors. In case they are not friendly, you get the weapons. Ann, you and Noah set up the household as we've done before."

"Is there that kind of danger, Jack?" Nell worried.

"Perhaps. Bloody Bill Cunningham has been harassing Whigs and may be this far north. We best be prepared."

Ann and Noah had already disappeared. Noah was running for the cabin where the weapons and ammunition were hidden behind a wall. As he ran he shouted and slaves came to join him. In a matter of minutes they would be armed and in their assigned places. They had done this before during the British occupation so all would be ready.

Jack swung into the saddle of Noah's horse and he and Ezra rode off to the south to investigate the intrusion.

Ann went to the anteroom in the upstairs hall and slid a board aside and lifted the exposed rifles which the women would use. They were light and, resting on the railing of the upstairs porches, would provide accurate firepower. Ann, her mother and aunt all practiced on occasion and were tolerable good shots. Within minutes Nell and Raye joined Ann and they moved to the porch on the south side.

Meanwhile Noah had armed and placed the slaves toward the area where the danger threatened. The hedge row around the kitchen garden would provide excellent cover for those with fowling pieces loaded with goose shot. That shot could kill a horse or blow a man to Kingdom Come!

In minutes all was ready and every eye watched in the direction where Jack Bixby had disappeared.

They waited.

Suddenly, those on the upper porches could see, in the

distance, a lone rider appear. Even at the considerable distance Ann could see that it was Ezra, and again he was pushing his horse to the limit.

Where was Uncle Jack? Ann wondered.

Ezra rode to the edge of the house and called up to Aunt Raye.

"Mis Raye. Mr. Jack say git ready to treat wounds. It's Mister Tom and some men."

"Who's wounded?" a concerned Ann shouted down. "Is it Papa?" For why else would they be coming to the Bixby farm?.

"No'm. It's Ben. A chest wound, they say."

"Any others, Ezra?" Raye asked.

"None I could tell. They all muddy and wore out from riding, but just Ben hurt, far's I could tell."

"Go and tell Noah to put the weapons away and have the young ones tend to the horses," Raye ordered. "And tell Hattie to start preparing the wash house."

"Yessim," Ezra replied as he hurried off.

Ann secured the rifles in the wall and replaced the boards carefully. They didn't need the weapons this time but there might be need before this whole thing was over.

When Ann approached the wash house the preparations were well underway. Behind the building the fires had been stirred to life under great pots of water. Inside the building, where only hours ago slaves had washed and ironed clothes, the large table in the middle of the room had been cleared. The wall of the cabin had shelves of herbs and potions. The wash house was used for treating injuries and sometimes a difficult childbirth. There was no fire in the huge fireplace but the stones were still warm from earlier use.

Hattie was wiping the top of the table. Used for ironing the large household linens, it was wide enough and long enough to hold a man of even Ben's size.

Noah had started the young boys carrying water from the branch below the bluff on the north side of the house. Each had a yoke across the shoulders with a pail on each side. As each boy emptied his pails and started down to the brook again, Ann wondered at the amount of water and for what purpose? But Hattie had ordered it and no one would question but that it would be needed if she said so. Hattie had been through this nasty business before. She had supervised Uncle Jack's care when he returned from Charleston in dreadful shape.

Ann heard the horses as they rode near to the door of the cabin and Uncle Jack strode in. He looked around the cabin and saw that preparations had been made. Soon the others appeared. A wounded Ben was being supported by Tom Bixby and Jamie McCaskill. Behind them came Francis Marion and Oscar. They nodded to the assembled women but spoke not a word.

Ann looked at Ben whose skin was grey and drawn. He was conscious but moved like a puppet between his supporters. He looked at the table as if it were a mountain and Ann wondered how he could be lifted to that height. Tom Bixby and Jamie McCaskill were strong men but Ben was a giant of a man.

Jack Bixby grabbed a small stool in his one good hand and pulled it to the side of the table.

From behind the three men, Marion's slave, Oscar, appeared. He lifted Ben's foot to the stool, then helped hoist the wounded man to the stool, then to sit on the edge of the table. Oscar and Jamie removed Ben's big, black slouched hat, his leather jerkin, then cut the muslin shirt around the red stain on his side. The bandaged side had oozed blood and fluid and the bandage was stuck tight to the flesh.

"The doctor removed the bullet after the fight but thinks it pierced the lung," Tom reported to Jack. "The impact surely broke some ribs. He's stayed conscious throughout it all and has stopped coughing blood, so the bleeding must have been stemmed. Of course riding through the swamp for hours didn't do him any good. That bandage looks nasty so I guess we'd best peel it off."

Hattie moved to Ben's side and nodded to Noah and Ezra who stepped forward and lifted Ben's legs up over the side of the table and laid him carefully on his back. Ben bit back any sound of pain but beads of sweat stood out on his forehead. His hair was matted and his face streaked with mud from sweat and dust.

Ann took a small clean towel and dipped it into a pan of cool water and moved to the table to wipe Ben's face. From across the table Jamie reached for the towel, squeezing her hand as she relinquished it.

"Thank you, Wee Ann," he murmured in a low voice as he smiled at her.

But the smile did not reach his eyes, Ann noticed. His face was lined with worry and fatigue. The young, teasing scout was gone, Ann realized. This young man had seen too much, suffered too much, grieved too deeply in the few months since she had last seen him. What other changes were there, she wondered.

Ben smiled his thanks, too tired and weak to speak. Jamie wiped away the sweat and dirt as best he could.

Hattie examined the bloody bandage that stuck to Ben's flesh. Jack Bixby stood beside her silently observing the situation. Then he spoke.

"Hattie, you cared for my head wound and bloody and festering stump. Ben is lucky to be in your hands."

With those words it was evident that he trusted Hattie to make the decisions. She had tended injuries on the farm and had healed his own. Now she would care for Ben.

Hattie stepped back and moved to the cold fireplace. She put a dipper into a large pot of freshly made lye soap, still liquid and slightly warm, and ladled out a full measure. Moving to Ben's side she finally spoke.

"Ben, soap's warm but not hot. That rag'll soak it up and soften. Then we fix that hole."

Ben smiled. After a torturous trip through the swamp he

was among friends. In his previous visits to the farm he had spent a lot of time talking of campaigning with the Bixby slaves. He knew them to be loyal to the Bixbys and to the patriot cause. They would take good care of him.

Hattie poured the warm soap over Ben's side soaking the material which clung to his flesh. She then carefully bent his arm high on his chest.

Ben bit back a groan.

Jack explained. "We'll bind your arm in a sling when we're done here. It will ease the pain in the ribs. Hard tellin' how many are broke."

Hattie stood with hands on hips and sniffed. "Ben, gonna keep the wound clean but you need cleanin' too. You smell like a wild boar what's wallowed in the swamp muck."

To Ezra and Noah she nodded and they moved to Ben's side. "My boys'll wash you like a baby and you'll rest easy. Need to find a pair of cotton trousers that'll fit."

Tom Bixby laughed. "We all smell like the swamp muck, Hattie."

"Sho' 'nuff, Mister Tom. There be tubs behind the wash house and the water over the fire's hot. Lots of water and lots of soap and y'all feel better."

Jack sent Ann to collect clean clothes and sent Tad with her to return with them.

Ann busied herself in the keeping room while Noah's wife, Jenny, brought food from the outdoor kitchen. Nell had the table laid in the dining room with the finest they had.

"The best is none too good for General Marion although I've not had time to meet him. Just had time to hug your Papa before they took Ben from his horse. When Ben is settled it will be time to welcome him."

Ann laughed. "Hattie already welcomed them with orders to wash. Told them they smelled like boars who had wallowed in the swamp muck."

"She didn't! What was she thinking of?"

Ann explained. "She wanted Ben cleaned and she told him he smelled. Papa allowed that they all did and Hattie agreed. She doesn't have any idea who General Marion and Oscar are. They are just there attending to Ben and she'll order them around like she does the rest of the household."

Ann reflected a moment, then continued. "But Ben seemed content to put himself in her hands. I 'spect she reminds him of his wife, Maudie."

The food was on the table and glasses were filled with clear water when Tom Bixby came in. He was dressed in fresh clothes and his hair was wet.

"Do I rate a kiss now that I'm clean?" he teased.

Nell obliged.

He then gave Ann a tight hug. "Wee Ann, you've grown. Soon I'll have to call you something else."

"Perhaps Sweet Ann would be appropriate," a voice from the doorway added.

"Jamie, how good to see you. Welcome." Nell Bixby greeted him. "I'm glad you're here but sorry about the circumstances. How is it going with Ben?"

"He's been bathed and they're working on changing the dressing. He told me to come to supper. He's still giving me orders."

"How long since Ben has eaten, Jamie?" a worried Ann asked. "Could he manage some turtle broth with barley?"

"I'm sure that would suit him fine."

"I'll go to the kitchen and see to it," Ann called over her shoulder as she fled. Sweet Ann, indeed, she thought as she blushed furiously.

When she returned to the dining room she reported, "Jennie is heating the turtle soup and it will be ready when Ben feels like eating."

General Marion appeared with Oscar close by. They were cleaned and looked much more comfortable after the harrowing few days.

"My wife, Sir," Tom Bixby made the introduction.

General Marion took Nell Bixby's hand and bowed over it. "Madame, I am pleased to meet you at last. Tom Bixby is a great comfort to me in these tragic times and I depend on his service. Also, I'm indebted to the bravery and patriotism of your daughter, Ann. Our service might have ended long ago had it not been for her warning of Rawdon's treachery."

Jack and Rachel entered the dining room and the two men shook hands.

"It's good to see you looking well, Jack Bixby," Marion remarked. "I'd heard of your wounds and I thank God you survived them.

He then turned to Rachel and bowed. "I'm grateful for your hospitality, Mrs. Bixby.

"We're pleased to have you, Sir," she replied.

Nell and Raye had heard so much of the brilliance and daring of this guerilla fighter that it was hard to imagine that this quiet, unassuming little man was the great partisan leader.

Marion then addressed Ann. "You don't look like a little boy in that lovely dress, Miss Bixby. But I'd not mistake that glorious red hair. I've never seen it except on a Bixby." He smiled.

Tad stepped forward to shake the visitor's hand. "Sir, when I'm old enough, I'll ride with you," he declared with certainty.

"You'd be welcome as Bixby men are great patriots. However, we hope to end this before you are a year older. Your service here at the farm provides Jack much comfort, and your father rests easier knowing you're here to assist your mother and sister." He shook Tad's hand firmly.

Ann left the assembled group to take food to the wash house to Ben. He was cleaned and the old bandage removed and replaced. Jamie was talking with Hattie when Ann entered. She had not seen him leave the house. Of course, she was trying not to notice him!

"Ann, you are just in time. Hattie thinks Ben should eat just a bit, then sleep. He's worn out."

Jamie lifted Ben by the shoulders and, in spite of his pain, Ben ate as Ann fed him the rich broth one spoonful at a time. Offered some bread, he shook his head. Probably he was too tired to chew, Ann thought. After a few sips of water, Ben indicated he was through. Jamie lowered him to the table.

Ben sighed. "Bless you, Miss Ann. Bless you."

"Rest well, Ben," Ann admonished. "There will be someone here if you need anything."

He did not reply. His eyes closed and he slept.

"He's hardly slept since he was hit," Jamie explained. "Thank God we made it here in time."

He watched Ben for a moment and, when sure that the sleep was peaceful, he took Ann by the hand. "Come. The rest of us haven't eaten lately and they will be waiting supper for us. Don't want Tom and the Swamp Fox to starve."

Seven

Bixby Farm

Supper was a pleasant affair. The food was plain as was summer fare. Cold meats of many kinds but, since the arrival of the partisans, the menu had been changed to include hot cooked vegetables. Pickles and relishes were added and bread. Lots of bread! The men ate as if they had not eaten in days and Ann suspected that was true. In their haste to get Ben to safety they had probably eaten sparsely, if at all. Now, safe at the farm, they could eat their fill.

After the meal, Marion spoke. "I should see to Oscar."

"No need, sir," Jack Bixby replied. "Ezra is seeing to him and they'll have eaten in the eating shed off the kitchen building. And the slaves on this farm eat the same fare as this household so he should be well fed."

"In my experience, that is not usually the case," Marion remarked.

"Perhaps," Jack replied, "but we have few slaves here. Most were at the wash house toting water, heating water or cooking. The adult slaves came with Raye as dower slaves and have been in her family all their lives. We have extensive kitchen gardens and the men all hunt when not working in the fields. We've had plenty of food even in the leanest time tho salt was scarce until you sent Jamie with a sack. Hattie hid it and it was used very judiciously, but it was used for all who live and work here. I think a man can not work if he eats poorly."

"That's true of an army, too, but the hardship can't be helped."

Jamie listened to the conversation and sat as in deep thought. Ann wondered what he was thinking. Finally he spoke.

"I suspect when I get back to the plantation I'll need to make some changes. We've had an overseer and gave him too much power. He joined the Tories after my father was hanged and he took some slaves with him, I suspect against their will. In this struggle we dared not trust but a few, while all of Jack's slaves are loyal. I need to talk to you further, Jack. I think I could learn a lot about how to run my holdings. I was away at school when my father died. I hadn't the opportunity to learn what I needed to know. I believed I could count on the overseer to run things. That was an error. When this is over, I must run things on my own and, after the conversation here tonight, I realize I have a lot to learn."

The talk of the future was optimistic but all around the table knew that the present was still perilous. Ben's wounds attested to that.

Finally, the men left the table and sat on the porch with pipes. They were served a small measure of rum as Francis Marion drank sparingly. As the daylight faded the deer grazed at the edge of the fields. Oscar stood outside the circle of men, watching and waiting.

"Buddy," Marion addressed Oscar, "are you set for the night?"

"Yessir. I've a tick of fresh straw and will sleep near Ben case he rouses in the night."

"Oscar," Jack Bixby interrupted. "Hattie tells me that they are making straw pallets to cushion Ben on that table so's not to move him. Noah will sleep in the washhouse and Ezra close by. They'll tend to Ben. They can rouse you if need be."

"Jack's right. Oscar has been at Ben's side constantly and has not slept," Tom agreed. "The colonel will sleep in a bedroom on the second floor in the house, so all will be safe."

Tom knew that by morning Oscar would be found on an outside upper porch where he could be sure of Marion's safety. The silent black man and the quiet little guerrilla fighter had been soldiering for years. Oscar was rarely more than a few yards from his master, waking or sleeping. On the trail he rode directly behind Marion watching for the slightest danger. There were many who would consider it a great honor to kill the Swamp Fox. He was wanted dead or alive by his enemies. Oscar was his shadow and any enemy would find him prepared to defend Marion to the death.

"Your laundry will be ready by morning," Jack announced. "Hattie had it washed as soon as you were bathed. They will iron the first thing in the morning so you can leave when you're a mind to. Of course, you are welcome to stay as long as you wish but I understand you have business in the PeeDee."

"Yes. Sad business but it must be done," Marion replied. He made no explanation and no one inquired further.

"Jamie, you'll stay?" Jack inquired.

"Yes, if you'll have me. The colonel will convey my regards and explanation to my mother. I want to stay with Ben until the danger is past. The wound is serious and a lot can go wrong."

"Certainly, you're welcome to stay. To keep an eye on Ben. Do we have no other attractions?"

"Perhaps. Perhaps," Jamie replied, knowing Jack's tendency to tease.

Francis Marion retired early, as well as Tom and Nell Bixby.

After bidding a good night to those retiring Jamie took Ann by the hand and pulled her from her chair. "Walk with me, Ann."

The two left the house and walked, hand-in-hand, to the cabin where Ben lay. He was still sleeping soundly as the two entered.

Noah stirred from a bench close-by. "He's sleepin' sound, Miss Ann. Groans a bit when he moves in his sleep."

In spite of the heat of the night, Ben, head wrapped in cloth, was covered up to his neck with a light covering. A small fire smoked in the fireplace.

"Hattie say keep a smudge fire goin'," Noah explained. "She want no vermin or insects near Ben. I feed green leaves to the fire so she smoke. Mornin' Hattie fix a fresh poultice to draw the pizzen."

With Jamie satisfied that Ben was as comfortable as possible, the two left the cabin and walked quietly by the line of slave cabins along the side of the yard. Voices spoke to them from the dark porches as slaves enjoyed the slight breeze which the night had offered.

"You should get some sleep, Jamie. Ben will be cared for. Noah is most reliable."

"I don't think I can sleep. God, what a week!"

"I know you feel Ben's wound deeply but. . ."

"Oh, Sweet Ann! It's the guilt I feel. That bullet was meant for me. Ben yelled for me to duck and I hit the ground. Ben stood and drew the fire, then killed the shooter before he collapsed. We lost so many men needlessly. Men like Ben should never have been in that line of fire. If Marion had been commanding there would have been far fewer casualties. He and Lt. Col. Lee wanted to wait for a field piece but Sumter would have none of it. He attacked and put us in the worst possible position. His own men were entrenched behind walls while we took the brunt. It was suicide. Marion has sworn he'll never again fight under Sumter's command and Lee won't either. Good men lost because of Tom Sumter's recklessness."

Ann's grip on his hand tightened. "When will this terrible business be over? How long can it continue? Reports are that the British keep retreating to Charleston but still there is bloodshed."

"Ann, I shouldn't trouble you with my fears, but I need to talk. When Marion ran a guerrilla campaign, it was hit and run and 'tho we lost men, we could control our destiny. Now the Continental Army plans our moves and the tactics are different. General Greene tells how important the militia are but has no real confidence in us. If we had a general like Daniel Morgan we'd be better utilized. He won over Tarleton at Cowpens by using Andrew Pickens' sharpshooters to pick off the officers and sergeants. We need a general like him in the Carolinas."

"Is there any hope that Morgan could come?"

"None."

The two walked on in silence. Finally Ann spoke. "Are you uneasy about Ben staying here when you leave tomorrow? You know we will do everything in our power to see that he recovers."

"I'm not leaving, Ann. Jack has invited me to stay on and the others will stop and explain to mother. She would understand that I'd not leave Ben until I was sure of his recovery."

"I thought you'd leave with the others."

"Don't you want my company for a few days?" he complained.

Ann thought a long time as they walked along. She had seen and felt the changes in Jamie. Now she understood some of the change. Although he was not the jaunty scout she had met when she first moved to the farm, perhaps he had not changed so much.

Jamie stood her silence as long as he could. He shook the hand he held. "Ann, will you be uncomfortable with my company?"

"Oh, no. I was just thinking."

"Thinking about me" he teased.

"Yes. And Ben and Papa and the rest," she replied somberly.

The walk ended at the house and they entered the foyer. "I hope your sleep is peaceful, Jamie. You need the rest." Ann told him as she left to go to her room.

"Sweet dreams, Sweet Ann. Sweet dreams."

Ann entered the keeping room to find Uncle Jack eating breakfast at the long harvest table. He was drinking a strong herb drink which the Bixbys drank in place of the British tea which some blamed for the entire war.

"Are you waiting for your meal, Uncle? I'll fix you a plate," Ann offered.

"No, Wee Ann. I ate with the general just before dawn. He and Oscar left at first light."

"Uncle, last night and this morning, people have referred to the Swamp Fox as "general" and other times as "colonel." I don't understand," Ann complained.

"Well, he is a brigadier general of militia, but has a commission as a lieutenant colonel in the Continental Army from his days in the 2nd South Carolina Regiment. He prefers to be thought of as a colonel since, if captured, he could be exchanged for a British officer of that rank and there are plenty of those. But as a general, it would be almost impossible for an exchange."

Ann thought of that for a moment. "Do you think there is any chance he would ever be captured. Aren't there too many who would kill him rather than take him alive."

"Yes, I'm afraid so. There is too much hatred directed toward the Swamp Fox. I expect that though the British say they want Marion dead or alive, they'd prefer him dead. But let us not talk of such a thing. Just pray that Marion will survive to see this colony free."

Ann was thoughtful as she ate. Yes, she prayed daily for Papa, Jamie, Ben and all those who rode in Marion's Brigade. There was little more a girl could do except pray. The days of her spying in Camden were over and Ann was glad of that. But she wished there was something she could do other than

62

help on the farm during the day and tend to her needlework when she had the time. She was safe, but it was boring. She wished she could ride with the Swamp Fox, but that was out of the question. She remembered her mother's admonition from the early days. Women could only wait and pray.

Uncle Jack's voice interrupted her revery. "You might fix a plate for Jamie as he just went to check on Ben and will shortly be back to eat."

"Where is Hattie? Is she not in the kitchen?"

"No, she left after our guests were fed and went into the swamp. She wants leaves for a poultice."

"She has rafters hung with dried leaves. Did she not have enough?"

"No, she wants fresh leaves. Says that the oil in the fresh leaves will draw the poison out. I must say that it worked on my wounds so I'll not doubt her."

When Jamie came into the keeping room his plate was ready.

"Just a few sausage, fried potatoes and eggs," Jack explained.

"Fine, Jack. We've been on very short rations and you can't imagine how fine it feels to sit at table and eat. And the company is prettier, too," he teased as he winked at Ann.

Ann blushed and got up from the table to pour more of the hot, spicy liquid in the men's mugs. Prettier, indeed!

Finally, Jamie and Jack pushed chairs away from the table and moved outside towards the wash house.

"Come, Ann," Uncle Jack called. "We should see to Ben and what he can eat."

Hattie was busy in the wash house when they arrived. The pungent odor of simmering herbs assailed their senses.

Hattie had smeared more lye soap over Ben's open wound, and had pulled a bit of the lint which had plugged the wound. Ben's face was grey and his teeth clenched. It was a painful wound.

Then, the soap was washed out of the wound with warm

63

water, and finally with water in which herbs had been simmered. Next Hattie dipped a clean bandage into the herb water and, after wringing it out, placed the leaves over the bandage. This poultice she applied to Ben's wound, covered it with clean fabric and pulled Ben's shirt down over the dressing.

Ben relaxed a bit and smiled.

"That will draw the pizzon out," Hattie declared. "Now, with some good vittals you'll be good as new."

Jack laughed and agreed. He pulled his empty sleeve back to expose the stump of his arm, scarred but completely healed.

"When I arrived in Camden the wounds were festering and maggots crawled over rotting flesh. Hattie trimmed off dead flesh and smeared me with lye soap then applied a fresh poultice every day. Sure did smart but it healed smooth as a baby's bottom. Do as Hattie says, Ben. You'll be right as rain before long."

Ann watched and listened. She remembered Uncle Jack's ordeal and the worry but he was right. Hattie's care returned him to health. She hoped Hattie could do the same for Ben. Body wounds could go bad and kill.

Hattie sent a young slave to the kitchen for food for Ben. When it arrived and Jamie started to lift Ben from his pallet, Hattie moved to his side.

"Mister Jamie, we tend to Ben. After a little food, I'll give him a potion and he'll sleep. It's too hot for a smudge fire so the youn'un 'll brush any flies or skitos off. Hattie'll see he rest easy."

Jamie and Ann left the wash house and walked along the bluff. Jamie seemed preoccupied so the two walked silently for quite a distance.

Then Jamie spoke. "Hattie is a lot like Ben's wife, Maudie. I thank God that we got him here. It was a grueling trip through the swamps and I marvel that Ben stayed in the saddle. I couldn't leave him with the sick and wounded at Greene's hospital in the High Hills. Even where there are hospitals, men have little chance of surviving in the heat, and filth and crowded conditions. And I wouldn't be comfortable with him left there. Only the brigade knows his value as a scout and a sharpshooter. To strangers he is only a slave. Here, among friends, he has a chance of recovery."

"Jamie, you and Ben don't speak as owner and slave unless others are present. Or do I speak out of turn?"

"No, Ann. I have nothing to hide from you. You are right. Ben has been my caretaker from the time I could walk. As I was an only child, my father was afraid the women in the household would ruin me so Ben was my companion. He taught me which snakes I could pick up and which to leave be, which mushrooms would kill, which berries I could eat. When I was older I hunted with my father and Ben and they taught me to track, to fire a weapon, to fight and to ride. When I joined Marion, Ben insisted on coming and he swore to my mother, standing by my father's grave, that he would protect me with his life. And he's done that."

Remembering the conversation of last evening, Ann nodded. Yes. Ben had done that.

Eight

Bixby Farm

It was still early as Ann joined her mother and Aunt Rachel at breakfast in the keeping room.

"Where are Papa and Uncle Jack?" she asked. She wondered about Jamie, too, but was not going to ask about him! "The men rode to Camden at first light. Uncle Jack had business there and Tom said he wanted to make the patriots' presence in the area known," her mother replied. "I guess he wants to make certain that any thought of Tory activity is dispelled. Jamie went along as Ben seems better this morning."

"Yes," Raye agreed. "Hattie says that Ben had a good night and the wound looks fine. He sleeps a lot and that'll help him heal. Drinks a lot of fluid but doesn't eat much. Hattie will take good care of him, you can be sure of that."

"Then I'll work in the garden some," Ann decided. "The heat is hard on the vegetables so I'll harvest some before it gets too hot."

"Yes, it will be a blistering hot day well before noon," Aunt Raye agreed. "I wished that Jack would stay home but he says

I fret too much. He seems in excellent health but I can't forget how horrible his wounds were and not much longer than a year ago."

The two women sipped their herbal tea in silence as Ann rose and headed for the porch.

"Mind you wear a wide brimmed bonnet, Ann," her mother reminded her.

"Yes, Mum," Ann replied.

After Ann had deposited the fresh vegetables in the outside kitchen, she moved to the laundry shed to check on Ben.

Ben was dozing when Ann entered but, accustomed to vigilance in the perilous swamps, he opened his eyes but remained motionless. Seeing his visitor, he smiled.

"Are you comfortable, Ben?" Ann asked.

"Yes, Miss Ann. Tolerable."

"The men went to Camden but Hattie and Ezra are close by if you need anything."

"Yep. Best Camden know the British ain't there no more. Any trouble there and the Swamp Fox will come. No messin' with the Swamp Fox and his friends."

Ann smiled. No, the British were not around to protect their former friends and that was a blessed relief. It had been a troublesome year when former friends were foes and all were suspect. But Ben was right. General Greene and the Continental Army were in the state and the British were being pushed toward Charleston. There were still Tory militia harassing Whigs all over the upcountry, but Marion would avenge any brutality against the Bixbys.

However, Uncle Jack would not let his guard down. The reaction to the approach of the riders from the swamp was proof that the household was still wary. A large group of horsemen might threaten the house but the escape route into the swamp was still an option. Ann had thought of the possibilities many times. She would not rest easy until every British soldier, and the Americans who wore their uniform, were out of South Carolina.

It was late in the day when the men returned, tired and dirty from the long, dusty trip. After seeing the horses were wiped down and cared for, they moved to the verandah on the shaded side of the house.

"Sure is a scorcher," Jack complained, wiping his forehead. "But a lot was accomplished, I believe."

"Camden certainly knows who the Bixbys are and what they stand for," Jamie remarked wryly.

"Yep. Even some of my old neighbors spoke this time," Tom commented. "When I was last in Camden none would look me in the eye but that was the day the Continentals took over and everyone was suspicious. Now that things are getting back to normal there seems a real desire to move forward."

Jenny brought cool drinks and the women joined the men folks and the conversation.

"Would you care for some food, Jack?" Rachel asked as Jenny stood close to the door waiting instructions.

"No, my dear Rachel," Jack replied. "We stopped at the Stuart's on the way back and sampled Mrs. Stuart's meat pies."

Rachel nodded a dismissal to Jenny who returned to the kitchen ."Whatever did you do at Stuart's?"

"Intimidated them, I bet," Jamie chuckled. "Jack is sure a smooth talker and I never knew if he was giving friendly advice or making downright threats. I bet Stuart didn't know either. If he's a Whig, it was friendly advice. If he's Tory, he certainly knows what will happen if he plans any mischief."

"I saw him when the British brought the prisoners back from Gum Swamp last year. He shouted and celebrated like it was a great occasion. I was sure he was Tory."

"He swears he was just trying to save his household, and was always a great supporter of independence," Tom explained.

"Well, I guess that is possible," Jack agreed. "We did what

we had to do to stay alive. Raye took food to Tory friends in Camden and it looked to others like we were collaborators. Guess we can't fault others if they did the same."

"But Uncle, he came to visit you and his slave questioned your slaves about your health and any possible visitors. I think he was a Tory spy and I don't like him."

"That was an eventful afternoon," Nell agreed. "When he found Jack out on the woodpile directing the coke burning, I thought our pretense of Jack being a total cripple was over. If Hattie and Ezra hadn't carried Jack back, fussing that he was too sick to be in the sun, Stuart might have been onto us. But with Hattie's fussing about Jack's fits and all, Stuart was fooled. He might not have been a Tory spy, but it was certainly a suspicious visit."

"Yes," Ann agreed. "He questioned me about Uncle Jack's recovery from his war wounds and I lied to him. I just didn't trust him."

"Well, his son Robbie is certainly an admirer of yours, Ann," Tom teased. "He told me today that he sent his warmest regards and hoped to ride over to visit soon."

"Well, he can save himself the trip," Ann replied indignantly. "I have no love of Tories even if they are new Whigs!"

Jamie laughed aloud at her vehemence and was secretly relieved to hear her opinion of the handsome Scot he had met that day. He had been less than pleased when Robbie Stuart spoke glowingly of his regard for Ann.

Jamie watched Ann's blushing face and thought of how much his feelings had changed in the last few months. Less than a year ago, when he had first met her and knew she was spying in Camden, he'd believed her to be a child of ten or so. As he had met Ann and Jack in the swamp behind the Bixby farm, he thought only of the intelligence she had provided him about the British in Camden. Occasionally he had worried about her safety and admired her great courage. How could he have not realized that she was in her teens?

Certainly, the shapeless dress and apron she wore disguised her shapely form, but her face should have given him the clues. She had bright, laughing eyes and a sweet mouth of a young woman. When she spoke of the situation in Camden, the firm chin and defiant stance should have alerted him to the fact that hers was not the passionate patriotism of a child. He watched her now as her face flushed with anger and indignation. Both Jack and Tom Bixby loved to tease and Ann had raised to the bait. What a lass!

When the women had left to attend to preparations for the supper meal, the men continued their conversation on the porch.

"What did you think of Robbie Stuart, Jamie? Handsome devil, don't ya think?" Jack inquired carelessly.

"Suppose so," Jamie replied, knowing he was in for some Bixby harassment.

"Guess you noticed that Ann doesn't think much of our Robbie Stuart?"

"Appears so."

"Wonder if she is sweet on someone else?" Tom Bixby mused. "Any other visitors from the neighborhood, Jack?"

"None I can think of, Tom," Jack replied deliberately.

"You may think you're fooling me, you two sly dogs, but I'm on to you," Jamie laughed. "Do you think I don't know what you're up to?"

"I'm not up to a thing," Jack protested. "You, Tom?"

"Nor me. Just passing the time in conversation."

After a long silence Jamie spoke with deliberation. "It is no secret that Ann is very dear to me. When this war is over I intend to make my intentions known to her, but I've made no declaration to her and I do not plan to. This war has been a brutal business and is not over yet. There has been too much killing, maiming and torturing and there'll be more. I will not ask Ann to pledge herself to me until this is over and I'd thank you two mischief makers to keep your opinions to yourselves."

Tom Bixby sucked on his pipe for a long moment before

he spoke. "I expect Ann would wait, if she welcomed your suit, and I 'spect she would."

"That is not my concern, Tom. I hope Ann returns my feelings but I'll not ask now. I will not have her pledged to me until I know I'll survive this struggle whole and healthy. It would not be fair otherwise."

Jamie's intensity signaled that he had given this considerable thought and his mind was made up.

Jack finally spoke. "I know how you feel. Had I not been married to Rachel I would hesitate to ask for her hand now that I'm without an arm. I know Ann would be as steadfast as my own Raye but you are right. And I'll respect your decision."

But not content to stop the teasing he concluded. "I'll run off any prospective suitors like Robbie Stuart."

Jamie shook his head. As irritating as Jack could be, Jamie had great respect for this man whose scarred forehead and empty sleeve were testimonies of his suffering. Jack Bixby could still find pleasure in his family and protect what was his. Jamie knew he'd be Jack's victim again but he hoped that Ann would be spared the teasing. He smiled as he thought of her blushes and wondered what she would think of this conversation.

Finally there was no excuse for remaining longer at the Bixby farm. Ben's wounds were healing, slowly but cleanly. Tom would be needed at Marion's muster at Peyre's Plantation. And it was safer for Jamie and Tom to travel together.

Jamie and Ann checked on Ben before retiring.

"Time you was goin'," Ben admonished Jamie. "The Swamp Fox needs our rifles. Ben'll be there directly."

"Not for a while, Ben," Jamie replied. "You are not to leave this farm until someone comes for you, or Mr. Bixby sends you. Can't have you gettin' lost."

Ann chuckled. No one was less likely than Ben to be lost in the swamps.

It was before dawn when the household assembled for an

early meal. The men ate heartily as it would be sometime before they reached Marion's camp.

There were mixed feelings around the table. The men were eager to get back to the task at hand. In spite of the hardships it was exciting and exhilarating to be on the trail.

It was barely first light when the two horses were brought up from the stable. Jamie watched from his horse as Tom embraced his family and felt a sense of envy as Ann kissed her father.

With a final farewell the two riders set out to Camden. From there the River Road would take them south to the High Hills of the Santee which were stretched along the Wateree Swamp.

The River Road (which the British called the King's Highway) ran from Camden to Charleston and crossed the Santee at Nelson's Ferry. Tom and Jamie had engaged in many attacks on British and Tory supply trains which traveled the road in the past. Now the Continentals controlled the road but it would be prudent to keep an eye out for any Tories. There was still Tory militia in unlikely places.

The sun was high as they rode. The sandy road rose away from the swamp and into ridges of higher elevation. Here pines and hardwood were hung with garlands of Spanish moss which gave a grey and ghostly setting. Great clumps of mountain laurel provided perfect cover for ambush as Jamie and Tom knew. They'd used such cover time and time again and would probably use such in the future.

But there were no Tories in ambush today. Birds heralded their passing and a few deer and fox skittered away at their approach.

Before long they were aware of the sounds and smells of Greene's camp. Smoke wafted from cooking fires and there was the bustle of an active military camp. Officers shouted orders at troops in formation as the training continued even in this remote forest. Beyond the limits of the camp, men were digging what Jamie and Tom knew were graves. These were for the dead and dying from the field hospital which Greene had established in this place.

Passing the hospital tents they encountered the stench of rotting flesh and fevered bodies. Jamie looked at the men lined in their common misery and questioned the cost those soldiers were paying. Surely wiser men would have found a way to resolve this conflict but there had been no wisdom. Now there was no peace, only suffering and bloodshed.

"Hey, there," a sergeant greeted them. "Where you goin'?"

"To join Marion," Tom replied. "I'm Cap't Bixby of his brigade and this is Marion's aide."

An officer appeared and recognized Jamie from the meeting at Fort Motte. "Heard things went bad at Quinby Bridge. What happened?"

"We took more casualties than usual. Tom Sumter commanded and he's brash. Not the way we fight most often," Tom Bixby explained.

"Where's your black giant who scouts with you, McCaskill?"

"Took a shot through the lung at Quinby," Jamie explained.

"Damn shame. He was a giant of a man. Heard he was a fine shot."

"Still is. He survived and is mending. Anxious to get back with his rifle."

"Guess a man like that is hard to kill," the Continental agreed. "Glad to hear he made it."

Tom and Jamie continued along the road. The word had been passed that they were allies and most Continentals now recognized the white cockades on their hats as insignia of Marion's brigade. A few had met Marion's men at Fort Motte and waved or hollered a greeting.

Jamie rode in silence long past the encampment. Tom respected the young scout's privilege to his own thoughts but he noted the serious frown on his companion's face.

Finally Jamie spoke. "Did you see the wounded?"

"Yes," Tom replied. "It was hard to miss the sight and the smell and the sounds of groans and sobs of suffering. They have surgeons with Greene's troops and they do the best they can."

"I thought of Ben. Hattie attends to his every need. Noah keeps a smudge fire going at night to keep the insects off him. When it's too hot in the day, Jack's young slaves with feathers and swatters flick the flies and gnats away. Ben rests easy with clean clothes, good food, and his wounds are cleansed and poulticed with every herb and potion Hattie knows. I'm grateful to your family, Tom. I doubt that Ben would survive otherwise. If he had been here, one of those graves they were digging would be for him."

"Perhaps, Jamie. Perhaps."

"I'm sure of it, Tom."

Nine

Bixby Farm

Ann was stirring the broth in the great iron pot over the kitchen fire. She had just raised the wooden scoop to her mouth to taste the liquid to check for seasonings when she heard the commotion.

"Massa Jack! Massa Jack!" She heard Noah shout in great alarm.

Ann dropped the scoop and hurried to the door of the outdoor kitchen. Noah was racing toward the main house as if chased by the devil himself.

Ann rushed toward him. "What's wrong?" she cried as she ran toward him.

"It's Mister Stuart. He messin' with Ben," Noah panted.

"Where?"

"At the smith," was the reply.

"Get Uncle Jack," Ann urged. "I'll go."

As she raced, she wondered at Noah's distress. Mr. Stuart was surely a Tory, or at least a sympathizer, but what could he want with Ben? Could he have brought armed men to the Bixby farm? Everyone knew the Bixbys were patriot and that

Tom rode with Marion. Could this be an attack? There was still Tory militia active farther west along the Edisto, but could they have moved this far east? Ann entertained all sorts of horrible thoughts as she ran.

Coming around the end of a building she saw the problem. It was not Mr. Stuart but young Robbie Stuart, a lad of little more age than Ann, who stood in the yard confronting Ben and Ezra.

"Give me that rifle, you black brute," he demanded as he slapped his riding crop against his leg. "Give it to me, I said."

Ben and Ezra stood across the yard, legs splayed and standing solid. Ben cradled his rifle in his arms and the barrel was aimed at Robbie Stuart's middle.

"Stay back, Ann," Robbie shouted as he saw her advance toward him. "Stay back till I disarm this slave."

He moved toward Ben and Ezra while motioning Ann away.

Ann ran between Stuart and the slaves. She turned to face Robbie Stuart and saw that he was in a raging temper. Not one to back down and with a temper of her own, she advanced toward Robbie Stuart.

"What do you think you're doing, messin' in Uncle Jack's business?" she demanded.

"Where did this slave come from and where did he get that rifle? Stole it, I suppose?"

Ann had about enough of Robbie Stuart. "Ezra, take Ben to a safe place and wait till I tell you to return," she ordered.

Ezra turned to move away but Ben stood resolute. Ezra took Ben's arm but Ben shook him off, never taking his eyes from the tableau before him.

Robbie's agitation escalated and Ann saw that Ben had no intention of backing down. He was not a man who would turn his back on danger.

Ann moved to Ben, although Robbie was trying to warn her away.

She looked at the pistol in Ben's belt. "Is it loaded, Ben?"

"Yessim, Mis Ann," he replied, still not taking his eyes off Stuart. "But it shoots very easy. Don't need hardly any pressure 'tall to fire."

"Give it to me," Ann demanded and Ben cautiously took the pistol from his belt and handed it to her.

Robbie Stuart uttered a sigh of relief but it was short lived as Ann turned and aimed the pistol at Robbie's middle.

"Stand back, Robbie. Move way back before someone gets hurt."

Robbie stood struck dumb with this confrontation and it was a tense moment as Jack Bixby came rushing up. He saw, but was not sure he understood, the situation.

A raging Robbie Stuart, red faced and simmering, stood in the yard with Ben and Ann aiming weapons at him.

"What is going on, Stuart?" Jack demanded.

Robbie started sputtering but Ann interrupted.

"He tried to disarm Ben and wouldn't listen to reason."

"Reason? Reason?" Robbie shouted. "What's reasonable about an armed slave? And armed with a fine rifle and pistol? What are you thinking of, Jack? You could all have your throats cut while you slept."

Ann's temper, which was sorely tried, erupted in its full fury.

"It was your friends, the Tories and the British, who would have hanged our men, and burned out our farm, if they'd dared. We have had much to fear from you and your like but we have no fear of our slaves."

"Now, Ann," Robbie tried a conciliatory approach. "I've never been a Tory or friends of the British. We just did what we had to do to survive."

Jack decided Ann could argue sufficiently for the clan so he turned his attention to Ben and Ezra. "Leave us," he demanded. "Stay in a safe place till I call you."

For a moment Jack thought Ben would disobey but the huge man only jerked his head toward Ann. Jack knew instantly his concern.

"Ben, Miss Ann will come to no harm. She is safe with me."

Ben backed away from the trio who stood in the yard but, not until he was at the edge of the underbrush, did he turn his back on Robbie Stuart. There was no doubt that if Stuart were to move to harm Ann, Ben would shoot him down where he stood.

Stuart shuddered as the two slaves disappeared. "God, Jack. How can you rest easy with that black brute on your place? Where did you get him?"

"He's not my slave," Jack replied. "He and his weapons belong to General Marion and he'll soon be gone. But he is capable of killing anyone who harms Ann and that was the situation here."

"Jack, you know I'd not harm Ann," Robbie argued.

"I know that, but he does not. A Stuart in a towering rage is not to be taken lightly and he was not to know that you are more blow than bravery."

Stuart did not dispute what was surely less than a compliment. He finally turned to Ann. "And would you shoot me, Ann?"

"Before I would let anyone disarm a member of Marion's Brigade, I'd pull the trigger. No one must interfere with the men who are fighting to drive the British from our shores."

Robbie knew of the strong patriot feelings of this young lady and had been made aware of her courage through the tales told in Camden. He also knew she was highly regarded by Marion's Brigade and her father, Tom Bixby, rode in that company. He breathed easier now. He'd heard that Marion's own slave rode with the brigade and the giant with the rifle was surely he.

"Come to the porch and have some refreshment, Robbie," Jack invited. "And Ann, may I have that pistol for safekeeping?"

Ann handed her uncle the pistol, and headed for the

78

kitchen to tell Hattie to prepare something for the men. She then joined Robbie and her uncle as they ate and drank.

When Robbie was about to depart, he asked Ann to walk him to his horse and, as the two walked, he tried to take her hand but she shook it away.

"Are you still mad at me, Ann?"

"Yes. Whatever prompted you to mess with Uncle Jack's slaves?"

"Well, I was worried about your safety. You know in the years we played together I've always wanted to take care of you. Now that Jack needs help with the farm, perhaps we should think seriously of our future. Yours and mine, Ann."

Ann thought of the uncertainty she had witnessed of the loyalty of the Stuarts. They may be friends now but were they friends during the hard times? She suspected not.

"I think it too early to think of the future, Robbie. The British have to be driven back to England and the country free before I think of any personal plans. And are you not going to help? Isn't every man required to serve in the militia?" She knew full well that Robbie had not served a day in the defense of his country.

"I intend to join Thomas Sumter's militia. He has promised slaves to those who enlist with him."

Ann knew of the plunder and loot Sumter divided among his men and she thought very little of the man. Robbie was probably with the right commander. A good connection she thought. Opportunists.

Ann walked back to the porch and sat quietly as Uncle Jack smoked.

"Guess Robbie bit off more than he could chew," he remarked quietly.

"Guess so. He thought Ezra and Ben would cower before him and obey. I doubt that there is a man alive who could wrest that rifle from Ben."

"But he gave you his pistol without a thought that you would turn it on him," Jack noted.

79

"I had to make it clear to Robbie that he had to back off. With the pistol in my hand I was safe and Ben knew it. That made it unlikely that he would shoot."

"But Ben would kill to protect you, Ann. Jamie would have expected him to take care of you as would General Marion and Tom. I don't think Robbie knew that Ben had been wounded and I hope he forgets this episode. I don't want him poking around here."

"He says he is enlisting with Thomas Sumter and will get a slave for his trouble. He'd also like to plan a future with me." After delivering this bombshell Ann fell silent.

"Ann, you have no interest in him, do you?" an impatient Jack asked.

"No, Uncle. Absolutely none."

"Then if he mentions it again, you have him speak to me. You're too young to even think of marriage." He shook his head in puzzlement. Whatever gave Stuart the idea that his suit would be welcome? Well, I'll disabuse him of that, Jack decided.

Jack and Ann walked around the yard and the garden area, keeping an eye to where Robbie Stuart rode away into the distance. Finally, when all signs of the horseman were gone, Jack called to Noah who came from where he had watched the proceedings unseen.

"Yes sir, " he answered.

"Noah, we must remain alert. How did Stuart get close enough to Ben to cause trouble?"

"He headed to the house. Then started to the outbuildings. Don't know when he took it to him to meddle."

"Watch more carefully. We want no one to take us unawares. Even one horseman is too many if he's bent on mischief."

"Yessir," Noah nodded in agreement. "We'll watch good."

"Where are Ben and Ezra?" Ann asked.

"Took to the woods, Miss Ann. Down the bluff by the old bridge."

"Ben should not be on his feet so long, and certainly not in the swamp," Ann decided, worried about Ben's recovery. He was on his feet but his wound was not healed.

Jack and Ann walked toward the swamp and stood behind the slave cabins at the edge of the bluff overlooking the branch of the river which provided water for the household.

Ann put her hands to her mouth and started the series of crow calls which would signal Ben that it was safe. Two caws- then one-then three- then one- and a final two. It had been weeks since those calls had signaled Marion's scouts in the woods but Ben would remember the many times Ann had met with Jamie to pass on information about Camden. She had no need of spying now but the signal would serve them in this case.

Soon there was the answering call from the other side of the water and Ezra and Ben appeared. Ezra hailed Noah who rushed down the bank to take Ben's arm and together the two Bixby slaves aided the wounded patriot in climbing the bluff. Although Ben had stood firm in the confrontation with Robbie Stuart, his strength was waning rapidly as he was helped to the wash house and his pallet.

Hattie fussed over him as she lifted the shirt and saw fresh blood on the bandage. Wringing out cloths in the ever-present potion she applied a fresh poultice.

"What you thinkin' of, boy," she scolded Ben. "That swamp air ain't good."

Ben's head hung in mute apology as Hattie nagged on.

Ann turned away with a smile. She thought of Hattie scolding a giant of a man who would have killed Stuart in a minute. However, Ben was gentle as a lamb as Hattie fussed.

Assured that Ben had suffered no serious damage Ann and Jack walked to the house.

"Do you think Ben is safe here?" Ann asked. "Can Robbie be trusted not to make more trouble?"

"We'll keep a closer watch, but if he thinks he wants to court you he surely knows now what's in his best interests."

"I suppose," Ann agreed as she walked slowly along, her thoughts far from the farm. "I suppose."

That evening on the porch Robbie's attempt to disarm Ben was discussed.

"He just wanted to show off for Ann," Jack commented, always one to tease.

"Oh, Uncle," Ann protested.

"You'd not marry Robbie Stuart, would you, Ann?" a worried Tad asked.

"Tad, I'm not fixin' to marry anybody," Ann assured him.

"That's fine, then," Tad nodded. "I'd not like you to marry him."

Nell Bixby observed, "Ann is too young to marry anyone any time soon, son. You needn't worry about it."

"Well," Tad continued soberly, "there aren't many good men around. None I'd want Ann to marry."

"Not even in Camden?" Jack teased. "Mrs. Kershaw has a brother who is about the right age."

"Uncle Jack," an exasperated Ann exploded. "I remember him from growing up in town and he thinks too much of himself. After Camden was evacuated he joined Marion but he is just newly joined. He spent the British occupation in Camden, perhaps he was a Whig, as surely Mrs. Kershaw was. However, I have no interest in him. Even Robbie Stuart is now going to ride with Sumter and pretend to be a great patriot."

"Well, " Tad start unequivocally, "I'd rather you marry Jamie. He's been a patriot for a long time and fighting with Papa. Yep, I'd like it if you married him."

Ann blushed and ducked her head, and her mother took pity on her.

"Now Tad and Jack, no more talk of marrying. We have years to think about that. Now is not the time for you to worry Ann about such things."

Nell Bixby was a quiet woman but both Tad and Jack knew

that she had reached her limit with the teasing. Tad fell silent and Jack sucked on his pipe.

Sitting on the porch floor, Ann pulled her knees up to her chest and wrapped her arms around her legs. She put her head down on her knees and hid her blushing face. Marry Robbie Stuart? Never.

But Jamie McCaskill? He was far beyond her station. His family was rich and, before the war, had lived like gentry. She wondered if she would see him after the war was over. He would return to the low country beyond the Pee Dee River and she would be here at the farm. She knew that even if she never saw him again, she would never forget him.

Ten

Peyre's Plantation

"What's happening, Jamie?" a perplexed Tom Bixby asked.

Tom had just returned from a sweep around the area intended to intimidate the local Tories.

"The British have hanged Col. Hayne in Charleston. Major Fraser's South Carolina Royalists took him prisoner and turned him over to the British. Lord Rawdon and Col. Balfour hanged him without a proper trial I hear."

Tom Bixby shook his head in dismay. "Have we orders to ride? Colonel Marion gave Col. Hayne and his officers their commissions. I 'spect he'll want to spread terror through the Tory ranks now."

"Not yet. General Greene sent a message as soon as it was known that Hayne was dead. General Marion has not spoken a word to anyone since the message arrived. He's in one foul mood, speechless with anger. I suspect that something will come of this with or without Greene's permission."

"I have no doubt there'll be hell to pay if the Swamp Fox has his way. Such wanton brutality is not his way, but if that is the way things are, Marion will not shrink from the task of meting out retribution."

There was little noise in the camp. Men spoke in hushed voices, their anger expressed in the threatening postures and grim expressions. What would Marion do? Someone had to pay for this. The consensus among the men was that they should ride against the nearest Tories and hang them all.

Finally, Marion called for Jamie, and handed him the letter from Greene. "I must respond to this although my heart does not concur. My mind tells me that the general is right. If we start hanging Tories in retribution, the British may hang the prisoners they took from Charleston and Camden who are safely in far away prison in St. Augustine. Greene thinks we should exact the toll on British officers and I know he is right, but my anger tells me otherwise."

Jamie looked closely at the little man who sat on a camp stool in his brush arbor hut and saw the anger. But he also saw the fatigue and the sadness. There had been so many setbacks among the triumphs and there would be more, if this latest development was any indication. Marion was not a young man, almost a half-century old, and he had lived in the swamps for over a year. He credited his daily vinegar and water for the fact that he'd had no serious illness, but the miles in the saddle were hard miles. And there would be more hard miles, Jamie knew.

My god, would this ever end?

Marion's opportunity to avenge Hayne's death was not long in coming. Greene's next message outlined the problem. The Tories were emboldened by Hayne's death and the Whigs were intimidated. Tory militia under Col. William Cunningham, 'Bloody Bill,' were moving down the branches of the Edisto toward Charleston to engage the outnumbered Whigs. Col. Balfour had sent the British Maj. Fraser and his dragoons to aid in this unfortunate business. General Greene had advised Marion of the situation and suggested, if his numbers were adequate, could he offer assistance to the embattled patriots in that section?

Marion did not hesitate. Here was the opportunity he craved. It had been Maj. Fraser and his mounted South Carolina Royalists who had led the raiding party which had captured Col. Hayne. They turned him over to Balfour and Rawdon, the British commanders in Charleston. If only Marion's brigade could get a chance at him! They would make him pay dearly for his treachery.

Marion dictated his response to Greene but it was a cautious response. To attack Fraser, who was moving along the lower reaches of the Edisto, Marion would have to move between two strong British forces.

There was great strength in the British forces in Charleston but Marion could elude those. The British Army which was encamped close to Fort Motte was a greater threat. That Army was on the west side of the Santee River, facing the High Hills of the Santee where Greene was resting his troops. The Santee, flooded miles over its banks, provided a barrier between the two armies, but Marion would have to operate between Col. Stewart's British forces and the Charleston forces. It would be a risky move but Marion, though cautious, was no coward.

"Jamie, I want the following militia alerted but no word of my intentions."

"Yes, sir," Jamie replied.

Jamie listened as Marion listed the men he wanted, and he was not surprised at the choices.

The men Marion chose to accompany him were seasoned campaigners and men who could be trusted not to desert and betray the Swamp Fox to the enemy. There were no former Tories, or "new Whigs", as Marion called them, among this select group. He selected men whose loyalty was unquestioned. It would be folly to undertake such a mission with any others.

The weapons they shouldered were a mixture of long rifles,

muskets, and fowling pieces. There were few sharpshooters and, of course, Jamie was among them.

As different as the members of this elite group were, there were similarities. All were superb horsemen, and all would follow orders without question. They had followed Marion before and would follow his orders to a man.

Jamie alerted the subordinate commanders as to the militia Marion desired, then left for a quick reconnaissance along the Santee. The British army which he had trailed before, when it was commanded by Lord Rawdon, still camped in the Fort Motte area well above where Marion was camped at Peyre's. Col. Stewart now commanded and he seemed to be settled in where he could monitor General Greene's movements in the High Hills.

When Jamie returned to Peyre's Plantation the selected militia had been assembled. Officers were checking every man's readiness for a long ride. Ammunition and some rations would be necessary and horses were carefully checked. Marion's men were mindful of the necessity of having fast, dependable mounts and great care was taken to insure that.

There was a quiet excitement in the camp. Although few of the men knew where their destination lay, they were aware that the brigade would soon be on the move. Supper was as hearty as the bounty of Peyre's could provide.

It was just sundown when Oscar brought Marion's horse and his own to the brigade commander and they mounted. The rest of the brigade mounted and followed Marion out of camp. Strung out in small groups, but still close enough to see the preceding riders, they moved away from the security of their camp and moved away from the Santee River, and headed west.

They rode all night, following the man they had followed many times before. Marion led the brigade through rough and untraveled terrain, along swamp trails and uncharted brooks. Wild animals noted their passing but not a Tory, nor a British patrol.

Marion was at home here. His own plantation was close by and his relatives and friends had occupied this area for decades. Known as the French Santee, it had been settled by the Huguenots like the Marions. The Swamp Fox had hunted and fished in these swamps as a boy and as a man.

When the sun rose, the brigade sought cover deep in the swamp where they rested, ate and tended to their horses. It was a quiet encampment as stealth was the basis of their previous successes and they remembered that now. No loud shouting, just very quiet conversation. Pickets were posted ahead and behind on the trail. They wanted no surprises. No company.

It was evening before they continued their journey, and they moved silently through the night. Daylight found them close to the lower reaches of the Edisto River, almost one hundred miles from their safe haven at Peyre's. Here they were deep in enemy territory but soon made contact with the local patriots.

After meeting with the local besieged partisans, Marion ordered his men to pocket their white cockades. It was important that Fraser not know that his enemy was the Swamp Fox as that fact might make him wary. And the success of the operation depended on taking Fraser unaware.

Marion's scouts determined that the enemy's strength included 150 Hessians, 150 British regulars and an equal number of Tories, all led by Maj. Fraser with his dragoons. It appeared they were headed for Parker's Ferry to cross the Edisto River.

With 200 of his militia and about an equal number of local partisans, Marion's band was not strong enough to force an engagement on equal terms. However, the terrain suited Marion for the kind of tactics he preferred. The British were strung out along the road moving toward the ferry which was approached by a long causeway. Maj. Fraser and his dragoons were well ahead of the infantry.

Marion was not certain of the discipline of the locals who

had joined him, but he had his own men he could rely on. He ordered them to line the causeway on either side and move 50 yards into the swamp. Reminded to keep their firing high on the horsemen so that stray shot would not penetrate across the swamp into their own men, the men waited.

Jamie stood well concealed in the swamp, and looked across the causeway where he knew other members of the brigade waited. He could not discern a single man and knew that their concealment was complete. The only men in the open were a few on swift horses which would provide the decoy.

If Fraser would take the bait and give chase, he would lead his dragoons onto the causeway and they would be crowded into a narrow passage. What fine targets they would make! His rifle was ready and he ran his hand along the smooth stock as he waited.

He could hear the mounted troops before he saw them. Their pace was measured until they saw the small decoy of riders Marion had provided for them. When shouts from the dragoons were heard, the decoy spurred their horses and rode swiftly past the waiting ambush, and scattered at the edge of the river.

Fraser raised his arm for an attack on what, Jamie supposed, he thought were local Whigs, and the dragoons surged forward onto the narrow causeway.

Jamie waited. The partisans held their fire. Not a man moved as each looked down his weapon at the unsuspecting enemy.

As the dragoons galloped past, Marion gave the signal and his brigade responded. Ball and buckshot smashed into the astonished troopers. Men and horses screamed as the projectiles found their marks. Fraser had galloped past the ambush and turned to charge his enemy in the swamp but the brigade had reloaded and he was met with a second devastating volley.

Fraser's only opportunity to escape was back across the

crowded causeway, which was littered with the dead bodies of men and horses. Wounded horses plunged and wheeled as Fraser led his men into the melee and met a third, deadly volley. The few survivors galloped madly back toward their infantry and safety.

After a brief exchange with a few of the infantry, which had heard the firing and moved forward, Marion signaled his men to move out and they moved back across the Edisto and rode eastward.

After about two hours in the saddle, Marion signaled a stop to rest the horses and for the men to eat.

"We could have took the infantry if we stayed," one partisan complained to Jamie. "You sharpshooters could take out the gun crew and we'd take the rest of them."

"You could at that," Jamie replied. "But there is not enough shot or powder to kill them all. When Congress gives us enough we'll finish the job."

After tending to their horses, the men ate their rations of corn mush and cold, cooked sweet potatoes, then rested. Before settling in for the night, Marion sent a squad back to check on the causeway and determine the extent of the damage they's inflicted on Fraser.

When Jamie met with Marion to write the report to Greene, the small patrol had returned and reported. By morning after the ambush, all the dead had been removed from the area and buried, but twenty-seven dead horses lay bloating on the hot causeway.

"Sir, we were not aiming at horses, but at the riders. If horses were accidentally hit, many more riders were down," Jamie surmised.

"I reckon Fraser lost 100 dragoons on that causeway," Marion speculated, "and we lost one private killed and three men wounded from the brigade."

"I'm sorry Fraser got away. Perhaps if Ben had been there he could have got a shot in him," Jamie remarked. "However,

100 dead dragoons for Col. Hayne ..."

"It's not nearly enough," Marion interrupted him. "No, Jamie. The 100 is only a start and it's not nearly enough. We'll have our chances again. The British thought that hanging Isaac Hayne would demoralize our opposition. Let's see what they think of Fraser's bloodied troopers."

Marion's men and horses needed rest. The long ride in the simmering heat of August had taken its toll on men and horses alike. The brigade stayed in the area assisting the local patriots in small skirmishes. For some units Marion had great admiration; for others, disdain. But he offered what aid and advice he could before heading back to Peyre's.

It was a tired brigade that returned to the safety of the plantation. They had ridden over 200 miles, bloodied Fraser's dragoons and scouted a large area of the low country. It seems that all this had been accomplished without the larger British force under Stewart ever knowing that Marion had moved away from his safe haven at Peyre's Plantation.

On his return trip he had learned that Col. Stewart had moved his troops from the Fort Motte area to Eutaw Springs and had set up camp there. It was too late to get word to Greene, but a message was waiting for Marion on his return.

"I told you we'd have other chances, Jamie," an excited Marion reported as he prepared to dictate a reply to Greene. "With the area along the Santee so flooded, Greene will have to go to Camden to get his troops across the Wateree, and then ferry the Congaree to get to the west bank of the Santee without encountering fire from British patrols. We're to meet him upriver from Eutaw Speings. He intends to engage Stewart."

With Nelson's Ferry at Eutaw Springs controlled by the British, Marion would need a circuitous route around that area. It was again a daring plan. Marion would skirt Eutaw Springs and Stewart's troops to the west, and arrive at Laurens Plantation which was about 17 miles north of where the Brit-

91

ish were encamped.

Marion knew this area like he knew his own hand. His home, now in ruins, was close by and he moved his men through trails he had known and loved to travel as a young man. The trails were remote and seldom traveled and Marion's men passed the British camp undetected.

If any Tories noted their passing, they did not raise an alarm. By now the word of Fraser's misfortune at Parker's Ferry was probably widespread. Tories who had sought British protection were increasingly aware that their allies were vulnerable. How long the British would be in the area to protect them, they knew not.

One thing they did know was that Francis Marion owned the swamp. He and his men moved around like the mist which swirled along the path in the morning, only to be gone when the sun rose high. But their disappearance was illusion. Like the mist, they'd be there again at dawn.

Eleven

It was a quiet night on Laurens Plantation where the brigade waited for Greene to join them. They had traveled up the Santee, bypassing the area where the British were camped at Eutaw Springs, close by Nelson's Ferry. There were no fortifications left at the ferry where Hessians once guarded the crossing. Lord Rawdon had leveled them as he retreated down the Santee toward Charleston.

Now Rawdon was gone. Had sailed to England, a victim of Carolina weather and the fevers which had almost crippled him. And too much Carolina militia, Jamie thought.

"What's the new British commander going to do?" was the question in everyone's mind. Stewart was new to Marion's men and they liked to know about the enemy. Gave them more spirit when they could make the fight personal.

"Don't know much about him, 'cept he replaced Rawdon," Jamie replied. "But one unit with him is the 19th Infantry of Foot, and we know them from Quinby Bridge," Jamie added bitterly.

"Yep," another remarked. "And we could of beat 'em if Sumter had let Marion and Lee plan that battle. Sumter be here?"

"No, I hear tell that he went to recruit in North Carolina after he couldn't run things his way any longer. Can't loot and plunder any more and that didn't sit well with old Tom Sumter."

"What's the word on Ben?"

"He's doing well. Seems the wound healed without festering. The lung will take time. Some ribs were broke but they are mending."

"I miss that big brute," another remarked. "Felt safer when he was firing close to me. What a shot! Could load faster than I ever saw and never missed a target far's I could tell. Will he be coming back?"

"Yup," Jamie replied. "It's been all they could do to keep him away now, but the lung's not healed and the poisonous air of the swamp would do him no good."

"That's a fact. Ain't doing none of us no good."

Many men around the fires that night were strangers to Jamie. Marion had mustered about two hundred infantry and about forty cavalry. Many only responded when Marion himself would command, and in this fight, Marion would lead his own men.

And others had joined the brigade, former enemies who saw the British withdrawal and now wanted to change sides. It was time to heal wounds and win the loyalty of those who had previously been Tory, but Jamie had mixed feelings about fighting along side former enemies. Would they stand and fight?

They were easy to identify. "New uniforms" the old timers called them, as the former Tories were better dressed than the men who had spent the last years in the swamp. The British had supplied their supporters well and they stood out among the ragged veterans. But could and would they fight? Time will tell, Jamie thought.

All the next day militia units arrived: Andrew Pickens brought more than three hundred militia and another hundred and fifty North Carolina militia arrived.

When Greene's Continentals arrived the total strength

swelled to more than two thousand. It was a ragtag group, Jamie thought, as he looked at marching soldiers whose uniforms hung in shreds. Many were without shoes. The units, according to the regimental colors, were from Virginia, North Carolina, Maryland and Delaware.

This Continental Army had fought at Hobkirk Hill outside Camden, had seiged Ninety-Six, and pursued Rawdon around Orangeburg. They were not without courage and experience, but they were poorly clothed and with a lean and hungry look. Many had stuffed Spanish moss under cartridge belts to keep the leather from rubbing skin raw. Were they ready for this fight? It would be a hard fight, hot and dry. In early September, the Carolina days were still blistering hot.

Jamie's spirits were lifted as the Continental cavalry arrived. William Washington, cousin of George Washington himself, rode in with his Virginians. Washington carried his own personal red banner which announced "Tarleton's Terror" and it was not taken lightly. Washington had engaged Tarleton sword to sword at the Battle of Cowpens and only fate saved the bloody British leader.

Lt. Col. "Light Horse Harry" Lee led his own Lee's Legion in with great flourish. They were splendid in their green jackets, white trousers, black boots and brass helmets with horsehair plumes. They, like their commander, were brash and bold, but they could and would fight, as Jamie knew well. They had been with Marion at Fort Watson, Fort Motte, as well as the unfortunate affair at Quinby Bridge. Yes, they'd fight.

And there was artillery: two three-pounders and two six-pounders. Fine for a seige, Jamie thought. He had no love of artillery although it would have helped dislodge the British at Quinby Bridge. Jamie would rather depend on the mobility of fast horses and riflemen to disable the enemy's cannon. But this would be a different kind of battle with far more men than he had seen assembled. And they would tether the horses and march into battle. Jamie thought this was not the way he wanted to fight, but he would follow Marion though the gates of Hell.

There was much activity at Burdell's Tavern that night but Jamie was not a part of it. He wrote a letter to his mother and one to Ann. If he were killed, they would be found on his body. If he survived, he would burn them both. They contained private thoughts which he could relate in person after this horrible war was over. But, if he did not survive, he wanted both to know how dear they were to him.

Marching orders came at four in the morning, and the troops headed toward Eutaw Springs marching in four columns. Lee's Legion rode out front. Each column could swing into battle formation easily. About three miles into the march Greene halted the columns and emptied his rum barrels.

Some men drank for thirst. Some men drank for courage. Jamie did not partake as he found strong drink only increased his thirst. Like Marion, he drank vinegar and water.

A brief drill was held in forming the battle lines. The militia in the front would take the initial attack, then the Continentals would move forward. Marion's men would be on the far right in the front line with Lee's Legion protecting their flank. Seemed fine to Jamie as he knew Lee's men would not falter and run. He wasn't so sure of other units.

As the march resumed Lee's Legion forged ahead and, after a time, returned with prisoners. He'd surprised an unarmed party of foragers hunting sweet potatoes for the British army. The diggers were run off and the armed party accompanying them captured or killed. But if Greene's presence had been undetected till now, it was no longer a secret. The whole British camp would know that Greene was marching rapidly forward.

Jamie heard the cannon as he rushed forward to take his place. He knew the little 'grasshoppers', loaded with canister shot, would delay the enemy till the militia could get into position.

Now the battle was close and personal.

Jamie settled into the rhythm required for loading, firing, loading again. Marion's line held steady even when the North Carolina militia to their left started drifting to the rear. Marion's line moved forward with a steady firing making every shot count.

The British volleys were shot high over their heads, and Jamie moved back only when the British charged with bayonets. His rifle was little protection for the bayonet thrust.

Marion had ordered every man to fire at least 12 rounds, but Jamie kept firing long after he'd delivered 12 shots. And every shot was well placed.

Soon the enemy got the range and gaps appeared in the line as men fell. Continentals moved up to reenforce the line and they held.

Suddenly there was confusion at the other end of the line and the British, thinking they had a victory, broke ranks. Then the drums rolled as Greene's reserves moved forward into position. The seasoned Maryland regulars fired a volley into the advancing British, then charged with bayonets fixed. Shouts of charging men and crashing bayonets were heard over the battle's din. The British line fell back in the middle and on Marion's right, but held along the bank of the stream.

Into this stronghold of British troops protected by an oak thicket, Col. Washington charged with his Virginia Cavalry. Horses fell under the withering fire and men, caught under their wounded horses, were injured or killed. Some who had fallen close to the British line were taken prisoner. Still, the cavalry drove on into the melee. The British fire continued and the dead horses and screaming wounded piled high in the woods.

But in front of Jamie, the British line had collapsed and moved back and abandoned their camp. Continental troops, thinking the battle won, stopped to eat and to drink. Officers who charged on ahead came under withering fire from the British barricaded in the brick house. They soon realized they had no covering fire as their men had stopped in the British camp to plunder. Food and drink assuaged their hunger but the clothing and shoes they found in the British tents were the prize to these ragged Continentals. Other units in the Continental army now joined in the confusion.

The British, seeing the breakdown of command, launched another offensive and Greene was unable to regain the initiative. He collected all his wounded beyond the range of the British fire and retreated. Marion ordered his men to assist in getting the wounded off the field.

As Jamie walked among the carnage, he saw Continentals and British dead, run through on each other's bayonets. Some dead still stood propped up by the bayonets which had run them through.

The wounds were terrible. Few of those who had survived the bayonet attack would live for long. Jamie knew that if he had to die, he'd rather a rifle bullet in the chest than a bayonet in the gut.

It was a demoralized group who marched with Jamie. It had been a hot and dry four hours but their canteens still held some water, most fortified with vinegar to keep it from turning sour. But they passed men who dove into the muddy ponds to quench their thirst. The ponds had been traversed by horses and men at least twice and were rank and putrid. Why were the troops marching the dry and dusty road when the Santee River was so close? Perhaps Greene worried about a British pursuit and wanted to keep the troops together.

When Jamie finally reached the point where Marion's men had tethered the horses, he was greatly relieved to reclaim Whiskey. The men mounted and, with the exception of those too weak to travel, they moved off.

Greene rested his bloodied troops at Burdell's where they had spent the previous night in far better shape and spirits. The dead numbered over one hundred but only a few were Marion's men. Two of the brigade's officers and three privates had been killed and several wounded. But the casualties were far fewer than at Quinby Bridge and the enemy had paid dearly. The brigade had shot more than twenty rounds each and they had made those shots count.

Greene prepared to move his battered troops to rest in the High Hills of the Santee. His hospital had been erected there and he had many wounded men and officers. Many would die there, Jamie knew. It would be a dismal camp.

Marion and Lee intended to stay in the area and keep an eye out for any movement from the British. That enemy still held the field but their losses had been considerable. Would they be reenforced from Charleston? Or would they desert the field and move down toward Charleston neck?

In spite of the new troops from Ireland in the summer, the British could not afford the casualties. Every British soldier killed left a hole in the ranks and few Tories were eager to fill them now. Only the most determined of the British supporters were still rallying around. Many had just disappeared as the area of British control shrunk toward Charleston.

That night Marion's camp was quiet. Men spoke in low voices, tired from battle and heartsick at the defeat. The field should have been theirs. They felt they deserved to win, but poorly disciplined troops had cost Greene the victory.

Tom Bixby sat with Jamie beside a fire. Nights were still warm and insects swarmed so the smoke from the fire was welcome.

"I 'spect you missed Ben today, Jamie," Tom observed.

Jamie took two letters from his weskit and tore them into small pieces which he fed into the fire.

"I'm glad he wasn't there. He makes a mighty big target and, without being recovered, he'd have suffered the long hours in the hot sun."

"It would have been a harder fight if the British had their own cavalry in the field. And Fraser would have been here with his dragoons if we'd not bloodied that unit. It will take some time for him to replace those horses and men. The campaign to Parker's Ferry certainly made today's fight easier for us."

The two were quiet for a time.

Then Jamie spoke. "It seems to me that this is no way to win a war. Lining up and firing and then attacking with bayonets. I think we'd inflict more casualties and suffer fewer of our own with Marion in command."

"Perhaps."

"Tom, you and Jack were in the Continental Army before the fall of Charleston. Were you trained to fight like that?"

"'Fraid so. It seems the commanding generals think we need to beat the British at their own game. But I agree with you, Jamie. I guess we are just skirmishers at heart."

"Tom, I've never seen a battle like that. Only one that came close was Quinby Bridge. Men don't seem to matter to those commanders. When we picked up the wounded, I saw men fixed on each other's bayonets. Each run through. Nobody wins in a carnage like that."

"Men matter to Marion, Jamie."

"I know and that's why we lost so few men in the early days of swamp fighting. He never would have ordered Col. Washington into that thicket. Who gave that order, I wonder? Dead men and dead horses in a great pile. Wounded men shot to death when trapped under their mounts. Washington and all his cavalry gone in one charge."

"Those closer to that action say that Washington was wounded and trapped under his horse but was taken prisoner," Tom reported.

"How many more times must we fight like this? I'm ready to ride and scout."

"Jamie, as militia you are only required to give sixty days' service. You've been in the saddle for over a year. Have you thought of taking some time for your own business back at the plantation? You've more than fulfilled your obligation."

"No, Tom. I'll stay to the end. You know I will ask for Ann when this business is over, and I'd not ask her to marry a coward." He thought of the letter to her that he had just fed to the flames.

"You're no coward, Jamie. Ann knows that well."

"When she was willing to risk all, she would wonder at my commitment if I failed now."

Jamie stood and reached for his blanket. "Best I get some sleep as Marion will want scouts out in the morning. Good night."

But it was not a good night. It was long after midnight when Jamie bolted out of his blanket and into the woods where stomach and bowel erupted in fury. Wave after wave of nausea bent him double. He shook with chills, then sweat with burning heat. All the time his stomach clenched in spasm long after it was empty.

He leaned against a tree, too weak to move.

"Jamie?"

Tom Bixby stood nearby. He held out a canteen of vinegar and water. Jamie took one sip but his stomach would have none of it and he doubled over in pain.

Tom touched Jamie's face. "You're burning up, Jamie."

"When I'm not freezing to death," Jamie complained.

"Camp fever. I've seen troops laid low with this complaint. You'll not ride as scout any time soon."

After reporting to Marion, Tom returned.

"Try to get a little sleep, Jamie. We're going to Jack's farm in the morning. We'll ride north and cross the Wateree. Then we'll head for Camden. Oscar reported that many men are down with the flux in Greene's camp so you'll have better care at the Bixby farm."

Jamie could only shake his head. "I'm not fit company with this."

"You'll recover, Jamie. But you need taking care of and Ben will see to it. And I'll see my family before I rejoin the brigade."

Rain had started in the early morning hours as Lee and Marion prepared to ride. They were to interrupt British reenforcements to Eutaw Springs or to slow Stewart if he should start toward Charleston.

Tom was to accompany Jamie who was now so weak he could hardly stand. After seeing to Jamie's safety Tom would scout along the river systems as he rode to rejoin Marion.

Tom helped Jamie to his horse. This would be a torturous journey.

Twelve

Bixby Farm

After frequent stops Tom and Jamie approached the boundary of the Bixby farm. Jamie slowed his horse.

"Can you ride a little farther, Jamie?" Tom asked. "We're almost there."

"If Ben can ride a longer distance with a hole in his lung, I can stay on this horse a little longer."

Tom peered at Jamie from under the brim of his hat. He didn't like the looks of the young scout. Nausea had dogged his every step and he was pale and drawn. He needed water but nothing would stay on his stomach. Without help soon, he would be in serious trouble.

"I don't want your household to see me like this, Tom," Jamie groaned. "Filthy and sick, I'm not fit company for anyone."

"We'll bed you down in the wash house until Hattie can get enough of her potions in you to stay the spasms. When you're presentable we'll move you into the house."

That allayed some of Jamie's fears but the thought of swallowing anything was not pleasant.

It was late in the afternoon when Tom approached the slaves who were working in the fields harvesting root vegetables. He spoke briefly to Noah, then rode on by.

Soon Ben was riding swiftly across the fields and met the two partisans. His wound was almost healed but Jamie was not sure he should be riding at such a pace in the hot sun. Jamie had not the strength to admonish him.

"Jamie, boy. You shot?"

Jamie shook his head, too tired to speak.

Tom answered. "No, not shot or hurt, Ben. Just sick. Terribly sick and unable to keep food or water down. Some sort of camp fever."

Ben rode close to Jamie and his face was somber. "I knowed I should have rode with you. See what trouble you gets in without Ben."

As Jamie nodded his vision narrowed and he fought to stay conscious.

"Ride ahead, Ben. Tell Mister Jack the trouble and tell Miss Ann I will see her in the house. Get Hattie. We'll take Jamie to the washhouse. He needs washing, clean clothes and rest."

"Yessah," Ben replied and rode off at a pace which belied his recent wounds.

Jack Bixby met them at the washhouse and helped the exhausted Jamie to a stool. It was a blessed relief to be off the horse and on solid ground.

Tom left Jamie with Jack who was giving orders to Ezra and Hattie. Ben hovered nearby, his face grim with worry.

Tom entered the keeping room and greeted his wife and Ann.

"You're not hurt, Tom," an anxious Nell asked.

"No, my dear. I'm tired and dirty but I'm well. It's Jamie who is ill."

Then, seeing Ann's worried expression, he hastened to add. "He's not wounded or hurt, Ann. Just ill."

"Then I should go to help Hattie," Ann announced and

started for the door to the porch.

"No, Ann. Jamie has camp fever and would be shamed for any of the women in the household to see him. His gut explodes and he can't hold any food or liquid. Ezra and Hattie will tend to him. I expect Ben and Ezra will wash him and Ezra's clothes will fit him. He'll feel better when he's clean but it will take a lot of Hattie's potion to settle him."

"But, Papa, Jamie is a gentleman. Should he wear slave's clothes?"

"Yes, Ann. The trousers and tunic are cotton and will wash easily. They are easier to manage until the sickness passes. Ben will see to things and Jamie will want you to visit when he is better. But now he needs no company."

"Yes, Papa."

Tom was right. Ben and Ezra had washed Jamie and helped him into cotton garments. Hattie brought a tin mug of herbal medicine. Jamie knew he needed liquid but it was an effort to swallow. He sipped some and choked as his stomach rejected it. Hattie assured him that a little would stay down each time. He was too tired to argue. It was easier to obey orders.

A pallet was prepared and an exhausted Jamie sank onto it. Ben moved his straw-filled tick onto the big table and stretched out, watching his young master. He looked so weak and vulnerable, Ben thought. And not so young as when they'd started this campaign.

Jamie closed his eyes and slept. Each time his gut wakened him, Ben was at his side. Before he slept again Ben ladeled out the medicine and Jamie choked it down. Spasm after spasm shook his exhausted body and only sleep eased his agony.

Jamie's sleep was restless as Ben watched over him. He stirred.

"You there, Ben?"

"It's me."

"I thought I heard singing. Beautiful voices. Thought maybe I'd died and was hearing angels. But if you're here this can't be heaven."

"No, boy. You ain't dead. Miss Bixby, Tad and Mister Jack sing on the porch in the evenin'. Sing church songs. Miss Ann has a sweet voice. Like an angel, I 'spect."

Yes, Jamie thought. Sweet Ann has a sweet voice. Jamie listened until sleep overtook him.

It was before dawn when Jamie woke again. He heard Ben's breathing and knew the slave was awake.

"Ben, how's your lung? And why were you on that horse?"

"Fine. Just ridin' a bit to keep old Midnight from getting lazy. Not hard ridin', but I be fit. Just pacing till you come. Time I got back to scoutin'."

"We're not up to that now. How is everything here?"

They talked till Jamie slept again, and talked more when he roused later. Jamie talked of the battles and of the confusion.

Ben told of Robbie Stuart trying to take his rifle and of Ann's interference.

"She aimed your pistol at Stuart, you say."

"Yessah, she did. Right at his belly. A raging fit, he had, but Miss Ann dint budge. One brave chile, your Miss Ann."

"She's not my Miss Ann yet, Ben. There's a war to finish. But after that, we'll see. We'll see."

Jamie drifted off to sleep and Ben stood against the doorframe. Yes, Miss Ann was a brave one. Jamie and Ann. Ben smiled at the thought.

It was morning before Tom permitted Ann to visit Jamie. She was in hopes that he might be able to eat something.

Jamie was still asleep when Ann entered the washhouse. She looked at the gaunt face, sunken cheeks and dark circled eyes. He'd been washed and his hair was bound with a leather thong low on the nape of his neck. He'd grown a beard since she last saw him tho it was not bushy like her papa's. It was full and needed trimming. He looked so much older than the clean shaven young scout she had met a year ago. She would come later she thought and turned to leave.

"Stay, chile," Ben spoke from the corner where he had been watching. "He be sorry if he miss you."

Ann turned back and saw that Jamie had stirred. He reached out to take her hand.

"I'm a sorry sight, Ann, but you are a joy to these eyes."

"Is the fever gone, Jamie? Hattie says you must eat."

He took the hand he held and lifted it to his forehead.

"See, my brow is cool. It is only the gut that is feverish."

"But food, Jamie? Are you well enough for a meal?"

The thought of food was more than he could tolerate and he dropped her hand.

Ben saw his master's stricken look. "Best you go, chile. He needs help."

Ann left swiftly knowing she would be in the way but determined to visit later.

It was early evening before Ann came again. She'd busied herself in the afternoon with her needlework. Jamie had been watching for her and had thought to send Ben to fetch her .

"Good evening, Jamie," she spoke softly. "Are you feeling better?"

"Some. Not ready to fight but some better."

"Is there anything we can do for you?"

"Yes. Please sing for me. I heard you last night. Ben tells me that you, Tad and Jack sing often of a fine evening."

"Just hymns, usually. Mum and Aunt Raye are afraid we'll forget the songs of faith since there are no services now. All the Presbyterian churches have been burned. But we had services before we left Virginia to come here."

"You can remember that? You must have been very young."

"Uncle Jack and Aunt Raye came first, built the house and then sent for us. I still remember Virginia but Tad was born here. We try to keep the faith and the hymns are important.

Also it helps Tad's lessons."

"Do you teach him?"

"We all do. He'd rather ride with Aunt Raye in the fields but Mum makes sure he is taught."

"So will you sing for me?"

"Not now, but soon. Papa wants us to sing his favorites at the house. Are you well enough to join us?"

"Not tonight, but if you sing on the porch I can hear you. Perhaps later you will sing for me."

"Perhaps. Good night."

As the Bixbys sang on the porch Tom added his voice to the rest of the family and the harmony echoed across the yard. Jamie listened intently and smiled as he heard Ann's sweet voice raised in the familiar hymns. He did not listen long as his strength waned and he slept fitfully. A worried Ben kept watch.

Tom Bixby came into the wash house and blinked against the smoking fire which was keeping insects at bay. He approached the sleeping scout and frowned as he saw Ben's care-worn face.

"Any better, Ben?"

"Nossah. Mebbe some of the potion stays down but not much. He be weak like a babe."

Jamie thrashed on his pallet and called out. "Papa! Papa! Run! Run!"

Ben reached for the wet cloth in a basin on the bench and wiped the drenching sweat from Jamie's face.

Jamie quieted and lay still.

Tom left the wash house and returned shortly with Hattie and Ezra. After a brief consultation Hattie left, then returned with a foul-smelling liquid with which she dosed Jamie as Ben held his shoulders up.

"We've used the last of the bark from Charleston in this," Tom remarked. "It comes from Peru and we have no hope of getting any more until the ports are free. I pray it will work."

Ezra waited in case Jamie should need help as he was now too weak to even stand with only Ben's help. However, Jamie did not waken and the medicine seemed to help.

Tom kept watch with Ben long into the night. Jamie's breathing became more regular and his sleep more natural. He no longer cried out. As the two worried patriots kept their vigil, Tom answered Ben's questions about the battle.

"Time I get back to scoutin', Cap'n. Time I get back."

"No, Ben. I'll stay until Jamie's fever is past and he's no longer in danger. Then I'll ride ahead. Jamie'll need many days to recover. He needs the best care Hattie can provide and she needs your help. Once his innards are settled, he'll have to eat a bit. You and Jamie remain here until Mr. Bixby is certain you are both recovered. It would be dangerous to go back too soon."

Ben nodded. He knew that Jamie was still dangerously ill. He looked at his master who was sleeping soundly now and wondered what the morning would bring. If the new medicine worked, perhaps Jamie could eat and drink. If not, there would be a dangerous time ahead. Men could go without food for days but not without water, especially in this heat.

It was early morning when Tom finally went to his own bed and left Ben keeping watch. Ben needed sleep but would not move from his place beside his master.

Ann's first question in the morning was about Jamie.

"Your papa says he seemed to settle a bit by early morning. He's still very sick," her mother told her. "Your papa will stay here until he is sure Jamie is over the worst."

"Mum, every day he goes without water and food he'll get weaker. What can we do?"

"You could eat and then see if Hattie has enough help in the kitchen."

Ann ate hurriedly and ran out to the kitchen when Hattie was swinging a heavy pot on a hook over the fire.

"Is Jamie better, Hattie?" a worried Ann asked.

"Kept some medicine down and a bit of water. Mebbe rice water will settle."

Ann knew that when babies were sick with fever and couldn't keep down their milk, Hattie cooked rice to a watery mush, then strained it and gave the water to the sick baby. It tasted bland but perhaps would nourish Jamie. Ann prayed that it would.

Ann paced restlessly as Hattie and Ezra made trips to the wash house. By afternoon she was agitated to the point of tears. Surely Jamie had to get well. He HAD to. How could God let a man fight the skirmishes Jamie had and then let him be sacrificed to a fever?

Nell Bixby watched her child with anxious eyes. She knew the pain of waiting and worrying about someone you cared for. She spent many a night praying for her Tom's safety.

"Papa, please can I help?" A distraught Ann cried impatiently.

"No, Ann. Everything is being done for him and you'd be in the way. I'll go and see how it goes."

Welcome news greeted Tom in the wash house. Jamie was still pale as a ghost but was alert and quiet. Hattie reported that Jamie had taken some rice broth and was able to drink water.

"Glad to hear it. I'd best tell the household that the worst is over."

It was welcome news and, as the family sat on the porch in the evening shade, they sang with happy hearts. Another burden had been lifted.

"Sounds fine, Ben," a tired Jamie remarked. Although he could now swallow some liquid his appetite had not returned and he was still weak. He nodded off to sleep as a relieved Ben watched.

Thirteen

Bixby Farm

"Jamie," Tom Bixby spoke quietly. "Ben and I will help you to the house, after Hattie has dosed you and you've eaten and washed. The women folk are distressed that you are sleeping in the wash house and not enjoying the hospitality of our home."

"I've been comfortable here, Tom. Wasn't fit company for the ladies when the bloody flux shook me."

"A bed has been prepared for you, and we'll help you to it. By the looks of you, it will be a long trip if you have to depend on your own power to get there."

"That it will, Tom. I can hold my food and drink now but I'm weak as a babe."

Tom was right. It was a torturous journey for Jamie as he moved from the wash house to the front verandah, supported on either side by Tom and Ben. They lowered him to a bench and he rested for a bit.

When he indicated he was ready, the two men hoisted him to his feet. They moved first into the front hall, then up the stairs to a front bedroom. As they lowered him to the bed, he sank back into the goose down bedding and closed his eyes.

"Rest a while, Jamie. Ben will have a pallet here in the house and can tend to your needs till you get your strength back."

Jamie was asleep almost before Tom left the room.

While Jamie slept, Ben moved in and out of the house, carrying the precious weapons and the equipment they carried on their mounts. This was a friendly house but Ben knew that Jamie would want his weapons at hand.

Finally Ben brought his straw pallet from the wash house and arranged it on the porch outside Jamie's room. He could care for Jamie and keep watch from here. When all was to his satisfaction he sat on a porch chair watching and waiting.

Tom reported to the family that the move had so fatigued Jamie that he was asleep with Ben keeping watch.

"Is that necessary, Tom?" Raye asked.

"Perhaps not, but Ben was rarely out of Jamie's sight and never beyond the sound of his voice before he was shot. Jamie will have all the help he needs. Ben is anxious to be soldiering again so this will keep him active until the two are able to rejoin the brigade."

"But not soon, Papa," Ann commented.

"Not too soon, Ann," Tom agreed. "Jamie and Ben were critical to Marion when we fought in the swamps. Now that Greene is commanding, the decisions are made at his headquarters. Marion still uses scouts as he wants to keep track of the enemy, but there are others now who can scout. Marion does depend on Jamie to write reports and keep up with a lot of detail we never had to worry about before. But that can come later. Jamie has been living in the saddle for over a year with little relief. He needs time to recover and it's best he stay here until he is fit. If we had been closer to the PeeDee I'd have taken him to his home but here was closer. Lucky to have got him this far in his shape."

Tom shook his head remembering the difficulties.

"I'll entertain him, Papa," an excited Tad promised. "When he feels better I can show him my games and read to him. Perhaps even play dice or cards."

"Not soon, son," Tom insisted. "He needs to sleep."

Assured that Jamie's recovery was well underway, Tom prepared to return to the brigade.

In the following days Jamie improved steadily. He moved around without help under the watchful eye of Ben. He and Tad spent much time together playing cards and rolling dice. Jamie taught Tad a few games he had learned from his father and found Tad a willing pupil.

The two walked in the garden and Tad named all the plants and explained how he and Ann cared for them. He escorted the young scout around the property and, when Jamie was feeling fit, they rode together for short distances.

All was peaceful at the farm but thoughts of war were not far from the surface.

Finally, as the Bixbys and their guests sat on the porch while the sun was still high enough to warm them, Jamie spoke.

"Ben and I need to be getting back. I think we should leave in the morning. If you have messages, I'll be glad to carry them to Tom."

"Must you go so soon?" Rachel Bixby asked. "Are you certain you are fit enough?"

"I'm more rested and better fed than I have been since I joined the brigade. I'm grateful for your hospitality and it would be a great pleasure to remain longer. But the country has need of us and we must go."

It was a quiet supper meal and then the group moved to the keeping room.

Tad, who had been as quiet as he could manage, suggested with great enthusiasm, "Let's sing."

Jack took a stringed instrument from the corner and handed it to Jamie. "Will you play?"

Jamie started to speak. Then, looking at Jack holding the instrument in one good hand, took it and started to strum. After a few bars he started to sing.

The verse told of a young man asking his sweetheart to accompany him across the ocean to a new land. When the verse was over, the older Bixbys joined in the chorus:

Will you go, lassie, go?
And we'll all go together
Over wild mountain thyme,
All around the blooming heather.
Will you go, lassie, go?

Jamie's voice was strong and true as he continued the verses. If that lassie won't go, the lad will find another and the refrain again:

Will you go, lassie, go?

Jamie watched Ann's face as she sang the refrain and wondered what she was thinking. Would she have gone across the ocean with one she loved? He thought so. One day he would ask her to go beyond the Wateree and Lynches river systems to his plantation on the Great PeeDee. It was a long way from her family and a different way of life.

Will you go, lassie, go?

As the song ended, Tad had another he wanted, and then another. The singing went on till almost dark.

As they stood and started with the preparations of shutting the house against the gathering dark, Jamie reached out a hand to Ann.

"I should see if Ben has everything ready. Will you walk with me?"

Ann rose and took his hand.

"Can I come, too, Jamie?" his devoted Tad begged.

"Certainly." And he held out his other hand.

The three walked to the outbuildings where Ben was check-

114

ing the harnesses and blanket rolls. The rifles, pistols and knives would stay in their possession. Even in this peaceful setting Jamie and Ben were wary. Always wary. Jamie wondered if ever a day would come when they could relax their guard.

Tad watched the preparations for Jamie's departure with great interest.

"Jamie, Aunt Raye says I ride real good. Couldn't I go and fight with you? I can tote water and firewood and take care of the horses."

"Tad, your papa depends on you and Ann being here to take care of things. Your Uncle Jack needs you to ride the fields and make sure everything is taken care of. They need your help."

"Well, you could leave Ben. He's been here a long time. He'd be a good help and then I could go with you."

Jamie saw the despair in Ann's face. He had to convince Tad that he must remain at the Bixby farm for, otherwise, the lad might do something rash like running away to join the partisans. There was danger in grown men traveling the countryside at a time like this. What calamity might befall a young boy?

"Tad," Jamie spoke quietly. "I need Ben. When General Marion has me working on reports I need Ben's protection. Many men depend on his sharpshooting and on his great strength. He can carry a wounded man from the field, and lift him up on his horse and carry him to safety. So I feel safer when he is with me. And I'd be obliged if you would stay here and protect Ann so I'll know that she is safe. Will you promise me that you will watch over her carefully so my mind is easy?"

Ann held her breath as she watched this exchange.

Suddenly Tad's face brightened. "If you need me to, I'll take care of Ann. Will she have to follow my orders if I'm in charge?"

Jamie laughed.

Ann announced with certainty. "Only when my safety is in question, Tad. Then, we will all follow orders."

Satisfied with that, Tad took Jamie's hand.

Certain that all would be ready in the early morning, Jamie, Ann and Tad walked back toward the house.

"Jamie, will you teach me that lassie song?" Tad asked.

Jamie started the lyrics again but this time sang with a faster tempo than before. Soon the three were marching briskly as they sang.

Will you go, lassie, go?

Jamie and Ben got an early start and joined Marion's brigade without difficulty.

Marion was encamped at a favorite hide-out, Peyre's Plantation, in the Santee River Swamp. Cornfields stretched out along the higher ground and the lower river banks were planted in rice. This plantation was, like the Bixby farm, well off the trodden wagon tracks on which the British traveled. It had escaped pillaging and had ample food.

Marion had settled in a cane brake. From there he could observe any approach by friend or foe. Here the men had built huts and had used the cane for thatch. In the surrounding area was forage for the horses, and corn, rice, pork and beef for the men. Marion found this setting very much to his liking and he stopped here often but never stayed long. Such was the life of these partisans. Always on the move.

Jamie looked over the camp and saw that the brigade was ready to move again although where and when would be known only to the Swamp Fox. The danger of a Tory spy getting into camp and learning the plan of attack was too great. Marion kept his own counsel.

But move they would, and soon, Jamie knew. Part of the brigade had already departed and, he guessed, Tom Bixby was among them.

Jamie left Ben to settle in and he went to report to General Marion.

"Good to have you and Ben back," the small partisan leader greeted him. "Are you both fit?"

"Yes, Sir," replied Jamie. "And rarin' to go."

"Much has happened since our disappointment at Eutaw Springs. Of course, the British suffered so many casualties that they have retreated further towards Charleston."

"Any action while I was gone?" Jamie asked.

"Little. We've not had enough powder and shot for any engagement. General Greene reports that he has none to send us. How does the Congress expect us to defeat the British and their friends without ammunition?"

"Ben and I have shot which were fashioned for us at the smith at Bixby's but we are in need of powder," Jamie reported.

"Till we get supplied we can do little but scout and trail the British movements. Our patrols keep the British from roaming too far from Charleston to kill and salt down cattle, and to keep the Tories from sending supplies into the city. Greene seems to think that is enough for now as he rests his troops. But Governor Rutledge has returned and I get messages daily from him. His orders will plague us to death. He has lots of ideas about the treatment of Tories. Wants us to recruit them into the militia and, for a six-month enlistment, pardons all their sins!"

"All of them?" an astonished Jamie inquired.

"No, not the infamous ones like David Fanning and Bloody Bill Cunningham. Nor the ones who signed the letters of congratulations to Cornwallis on his 'great victory' over the patriots," a disgusted Marion retorted.

"That includes the councilmen of Charleston," Jamie recalled. "And what about those who have been wining and dining the British in the city?"

"Suppose Rutledge can't exclude all those for I suspect that's the greater part of Charleston. Guess they'll play the role of great patriots when this is over."

Marion fell silent.

Jamie was surprised that the taciturn leader had spoken so bluntly. Marion was usually remote and quiet.

Jamie went to the general's tent and started on the reports.

Jamie was right. In the morning the few left in the brigade crossed the Santee River and headed for Cantey's Plantation.

"Good to see you looking fit, Jamie," Tom Bixby greeted him as they met at the new camp. "How were things at the farm?"

"Fine, Tom," Jamie replied. "I've letters from Mrs. Bixby and Ann for you."

He reached into his shirt and withdrew the papers he had carried.

After Tom finished reading, Jamie asked. "Anything happenin' on this side of the Santee?"

"Nothing much. Intimidating a few Tories is all," Tom replied. "When Greene sends us ammunition I 'spect we'll have more excitement. Most of the militia have been sent home to rest. No use feedin' them when there's no powder."

Jamie looked over the message from General Nathanael Greene and called to his superior.

"General Marion, there is good news from General Greene."

Marion limped over to the small table which was set up as his headquarters at Cantey's plantation.

"Better we get news from Greene than more directives from the governor," he remarked.

Marion sat heavily in a chair, his fatigue from the long campaign evident. "What is it?"

"Greene wanted to share the good news that the French fleet had arrived in the Chesapeake with twenty-eight ships and six thousand troops. Also, General Washington has moved south and is coordinating the activities.

Marion paused. "If I were Cornwallis, I'd leave Virginia and head south to Charleston where there are more sympathizers. And, if that were to happen, I'd take the road through the Cheraws."

"Then, we'd be in the thick of it again, sir," Jamie commented.

"We must be on the watch, I need scouts along the border."

"Should Ben and I be ready to ride?"

"Not yet. We have time and I'd not muster the brigade until necessary. The men suffered a brutal summer and a busy fall. They need rest, and so do the horses."

Fourteen

The Hurricane

The storm awakened Ann. The wind howled through the trees and rain slashed at the windows. Lightning flashes lighted the room as clear as day 'tho it must have been close to midnight. She pulled a wrap around her gown and padded along the doors leading to the upstairs porch. When she was satisfied that all were closed tight against the storm, she went downstairs.

"Who's there?" her Aunt Raye's voice called.

"Ann, Aunt Raye," she answered. "I'm just checking the doors and windows. The thunder sounds like it will be a great storm and the wind is fierce."

"It awakened me, too," Aunt Raye explained. "All the windows and doors are secure on this floor. I hope the fire in the outdoor kitchen is well banked. It is such a bother to start a fire when we lose the embers."

"I'm sure Hattie has seen to it, but do you want me to go and see?"

"No, Ann. You need not get a soaking on a night like this. Go back to bed."

"It's hard to sleep with the thunder rolling. I wonder where Papa and Jamie are tonight. Jamie is too soon over the camp fever to be out on a night like this."

"Don't fret, Ann," Raye replied. "General Marion has lots of friends who will give shelter from the storm."

Ann was not comforted by the thought. There were too many dangers in the swamps where the patriots fought. The swamp was perilous in the summer heat, but now in the first days of October, it would be damp and chilly.

"But it's not just the rain, Aunt Raye. The wind will chill to the bone."

"They will take care, Ann. Go to bed."

Ann did as her aunt bade but sleep did not come easy.

Ann awakened to a sullen morning. The rain had stopped but there was a heaviness to the air.

Hattie had been vigilant in tending the fire in the kitchen so there was hot porridge as well as eggs and bacon and hot herb tea. Ann sat with her Uncle and ate with a good appetite.

"I'll have Noah saddle Boots, Uncle. That horse needs exercise and I need to get out and ride. Is there anything I should check?"

"Yes, Ann. I reckon it would be wise to check that low pasture close to the stream and see if the water is still standing. The drainage there is not always good. If you ride that way take a look."

Ann nodded in agreement and left for the horse barn.

When Boots was saddled, Noah held the bridle as Ann mounted. Boots seemed skittish, Ann thought.

"Miz Ann, ride careful. All the hosses be spooked dis mornin'. Boots ain't the only one. Storm, I reckon."

"I'll keep a tight rein, Noah," she replied.

It was a strange morning, Ann thought. There were few birds about and the air was still and heavy. Quite different than the howling wind of the night before. Boots seemed to settle as they rode. The ground was soft beneath the horse's hooves and Boots pranced and galloped with great style.

Ann was reluctant to finish her ride but there was work to be done.

"The lower field is flooded, Uncle. The water is backed up behind the beaver dam and has spilled into the field. Should I tell Noah to go and break the dam?"

"No, Ann. We want to trap the beavers later. Can the field be drained by a furrow leading below the dam?"

"I believe so. It would only be a few yards if they furrowed across the rows at the edge of the field."

"I'll have Noah tend to it."

Ann wandered through the house and finally came to the kitchen where Hattie was churning butter.

"I'll churn, Hattie," a restless Ann decided.

She sat on the stool beside the crockery churn and lifted the handle up and down. To keep the proper rhythm for the paddle, she chanted:

Come, butter, come.
Come, butter, come.
Johnny's waiting at the gate,
And he wants his butter cake.
Come, butter, come.

Ann sat on her stool and worked the paddle till the butter had made, then scooped the wads of butter out into a wooden trough of fresh water.

"I'll work the butter, Hattie," Ann announced.

She took a small paddle and worked water through the butter to remove the milk which would sour the butter if left. When the last water was clear, she formed the butter into a great pat.

"Should I add salt to this, Hattie?" she asked.

"Just to part, Miz Nell say. What's for now, we keep sweet."

Ann divided the pat and to one she added the salt which had been carefully hidden away. General Marion had sent bags of salt which he had captured at Georgetown and the Bixbys were grateful. Salt was more precious than gold and needed to prepare and preserve food, and the British had tried to control it all. Even with the British gone, salt was scarce and was used judiciously.

"I'd wondered where you'd gotten to, Ann," Ann's mother commented as she entered the kitchen. "Thought you might take this dark day to work on your needlework."

"No, Mum," Ann explained. "It's too dark and dank. The air is heavy. Almost like the miasma of the swamp in summer. Don't you feel it?"

"It is a strange day," Nell Bixby allowed.

It was mid afternoon when the sky suddenly changed to a strange greenish tint. Suddenly there was not a sound. Not a bird tweeted. Nothing moved.

Jack Bixby laid down his pipe at his desk where he was working and walked out to the porch. He stood watching the sky for a few minutes, then called for Ezra.

"Yessuh," Ezra called as he approached the porch at a run.

"What do you make of that sky?" Jack Bixby asked.

"Don't like it, t'all," Ezra replied. "Looks like a powerful big storm abrewing."

"Think you're right," Jack Bixby agreed. "Think we may be in for a great windstorm. Best get the storm cellars ready."

Tad was called and, with a few of the young boys, was sent with torches to be sure there were no snakes or vermin in the caves in the bank below the house. They had used those caves to hide food. Now they would provide shelter for the household if the wind storm should come.

"Where is Noah?" Jack asked.

"Took four boys to drain the field," he was told.

"I'll get them, Uncle," Ann promised.

As Ann raced to the horse barn the wind suddenly rose with a terrible blast. When Boots was saddled she mounted and took the leads of two unsaddled horses. There was no time to lose.

Ann met Noah and the four young boys as they were heading toward the farm, tools on their shoulders, running as fast as they could.

Ann reined the horses in and Noah put two boys on each horse.

"Hang tight to the mane and to each other," Ann ordered.

Noah gathered all the tools and turned toward the farm.

"There's not time, Noah," Ann decided. "Drop the tools and get up on this horse."

Noah dropped the tools and stepped on them to push them into the soft earth. Ann pushed her foot out of the stirrup and Noah mounted the horse behind her, sitting on Boots rump and holding fast to the saddle blanket. Ann handed him the leads of the two horses and they galloped for the farm.

In the brief time they were gone the wind had increased its fury.

The shutters of the house were closed and the fires all extinguished. Everything that could be blown was battened down and the members of the household were hurrying toward the caves.

Uncle Jack was in the middle of the yard barking out orders.

"Noah, take care of those horses. Ann, take those boys and get down to the caves."

"Can't I help, Uncle?" Ann insisted.

"No, time is running out. Get to the shelter."

Ann herded the four young slaves down the slope as the rains came. Suddenly it was dark as night and cold. Ann pushed her way into the cave and was wrapped in a dry quilt which her mother held.

"You're soaked, Ann. Hope this will warm you."

Candles were lighted as the door was slammed shut against

the wind and the rain.

"Where is your Uncle Jack, Ann?" a worried Raye asked.

"I think he went into the other cave. He was behind me coming down the slope."

Ann shivered in the quilt and her mother hugged her close.

How long they would have to stay there was uncertain but all wondered.

As the wind howled, the sounds of trees snapping under the strain were heard, and the dull thump of trees falling. Ann wondered about the house at the edge of the bluff and if it would stand against such force.

And Papa? Where was he? And Jamie? Was he out in this storm? How could men and horses survive this wind and rain? She thought of her own Boots and wondered what Noah had done to protect the horses.

"Would you sing, Ann?" Aunt Rachel asked.

Ann started a sacred song which had comforted her since childhood. She thought her voice weak and wished for the support of Uncle Jack's strong voice, but she did the best she could. Soon Tad's voice joined Ann's. He was sitting on a wooden keg with his arms around his knees. His voice was not strong but he sang with enthusiasm. Ann switched to some ditties which Tad knew well, and the assembled group listened and enjoyed.

Soon, one after another, the children dropped off to sleep. Finally, the adults dozed.

It seemed late in the night that the quiet came. Ann roused and moved to the door. When all she could discern was silence she opened the door and peered out.

"Uncle Jack," she called when she heard voices outside.

"Yes, Ann. Stay where you are. We're just checking on the livestock and buildings, but it's not safe yet. This may just be the lull in a hurricane and another wind and rain storm may follow. How is everyone in that shelter?"

"Asleep, I guess. No one seems to be stirring."

"Close the door, Ann, and settle down. I 'spect we'd best stay here till morning."

Ann did as Uncle Jack bade and bundled up in her quilt and went back to sleep.

The household awoke to a strange morning. It was still. Not a blade of grass moved, and not a leaf shivered in the morning light.

Ann hurried out of the shelter and up the bank. Uncle Jack was barking orders to slaves who were moving about the yard.

When he spotted Ann he shouted, "Ann, check the house but don't light any fires until we check the chimneys. Ezra will check the kitchen and, if that chimney is sound, we'll start a fire there for cooking."

Ann rushed to the house and saw that the shutters were still over the windows and there appeared to be no damage except a branch or two leaning against the roof. Running from room to room she checked for water but found the doors and windows had stood fast against the wind and the rain.

Stepping out to the back porch she saw herds of deer, rabbits and wild turkeys milling about the fields beyond the kitchen garden. They appeared stunned and disoriented.

The garden structures were awry with the grape arbor atilt. Beyond the garden, branches were down and trees felled as if whipped by a furious wind.

Aunt Raye and her mother arrived at the house and looked over the premises.

"It seems we were fortunate in the house," Aunt Raye observed. "I hope the outbuildings stood as well."

Ann walked across the yard to the horse barn to check on Boots.

"He's fine, Miz Ann," Noah assured her. "Just spooked."

Ann patted her horse and saw that he trembled from shock and fear. Other horses were milling about the corrals but none seemed injured.

"Any damage, Uncle Jack?" she asked when she finally came abreast of her rapidly moving uncle.

"Not too much. Some shingles off some cabins and a little roof damage. Looks like the garden will need some work. Ezra is checking to be sure the wind didn't weaken the chimneys. We need fire in the fireplaces as every room and every cabin is damp. It will be a cold night, I fear."

"There are deer, rabbits and turkeys in the fields beyond the garden. They seem to be confused."

"They're that, to be sure. It was surely a hurricane and that effects wild beasts as well as our livestock."

In the next few days Ann and Tad worked in the garden to straighten the bean towers, move the debris and harvest the late fall vegetables which had been damaged. The men worked to replace the garden fence and the grape arbor. It was not long before the farm was in fine shape again.

In the next week a rider appeared riding toward the PeeDee and stopped to leave messages from Tom Bixby. There was another message for Ann.

She moved to the garden hut and opened the letter.

My Dear Ann,

Our thoughts were of you when the big storm struck. The brush arbor huts came crashing down but we took shelter in our host's barn so were safe. Ewen kept the horses with us so they are fit and unhurt.

I am grateful to you and your family for caring for me during my illness. I hope to spend more time with you later when this is over and I'm feeling fit.

Be careful, Ann, and keep safe. I pray God to care for you in my absence.

Jamie

Ann folded the letter carefully and took it to her room. There she hid it among her treasures.

Fifteen

Cantey's Plantation

Jamie was not a patient man. When would Marion muster the militia? Certainly he was without sufficient ammunition, but shouldn't they be ready to ride? What if Cornwallis and Tarleton made a break for Charleston? Would they have time to get the brigade in place?

It seemed General Greene was not unduly worried. He wrote almost daily reports and Marion was not pleased with the amount of time required to respond to them. And there were the governor's directives. Jamie now was called upon to keep abreast of the communications and to respond.

A welcome break came when a partisan rode in from the Cheraw area. He'd come through Camden and, being an old acquaintance of Jack Bixby, had passed the night at the Bixby farm. He brought letters to Tom and to Jamie.

Dear Friend,

Jamie read and smiled at the salutation. Friend, indeed!

He continued to read:

> We were happy that you suffered no ill from the recent storm. Our farm was spared serious damage – just a few shingles off the roof and the garden fence was leveled. Dad and I have been working to right the supports for the vines. The animals have been so confused that they wander in the fields as if lost. We thank God that we were spared greater misfortune.
>
> Uncle Jack heard from Camden that there was serious damage to the shipping at the port in Wilmington.

Jamie felt a great sense of satisfaction at that news since the shipping was British as they still occupied that city. Even the mighty Cornwallis could not escape nature's wrath.

> Dad wanted me to tell you that he has learned all the verses to what he calls your 'lassie song' and is eagerly awaiting your next visit so he can sing it with you.
>
> We pray that God will keep you all safe.
>
> Your friend,
>
> A. B.

Marion did muster the militia a few days later, still anxious about what was happening in Virginia. It was only with the arrival of "Light Horse Harry" Lee, who had been sent to confer with Washington's Army, that Marion seemed content. Col. Lee brought with him the news of the surrender of Cornwallis at Yorktown.

"Imagine, Jamie," an excited Tom Bixby related. "Imagine. Over 7,000 British soldiers surrendered by Cornwallis as

130

well as sailors and camp followers."

"And Tarleton? Did he escape?" Jamie asked anxiously.

"No, he surrendered at Gloucester Point across the bay from Yorktown. Seems Cornwallis tried to ferry his troops across the York River at night and a terrible storm blew in and ended that. So Tarleton was left to surrender his bloody troopers."

"What happens here in South Carolina now, I wonder," a pensive Jamie asked.

Marion was much relieved, as Jamie could tell. What also had arrived with Lee was a copy of minutes of Congress which contained a resolution to thank General Marion for his conduct in defending his country. It listed engagements in which Marion had showed great leadership, one of which was the campaign against Fraser's dragoons. Jamie knew that the copy would not be widely discussed as Marion was a private man, but it was evidence that his efforts had not gone unnoticed.

The next evening General Marion gave a ball for the officers, and their ladies who were present, at the home of John Cantey. He wanted to express his appreciation but he was not a social man. His gaiety was subdued, Jamie noticed, as he watched the Swamp Fox from the edge of the ballroom.

Jamie's presence at the ball was a courtesy. He was a scout, not an officer. However, he was the owner of a large plantation and, as such, he was considered a social equal.

Tom Bixby moved to Jamie's side. "A fine ball. I wish my Nell was here to enjoy it. And Ann, too."

"Yes, certainly Ann, too," Jamie agreed.

" I see some young ladies eyeing you, Jamie. You being the youngest and handsomest of the group," Tom teased.

"I'm not interested in these young women, Tom," Jamie argued.

The hostess of the evening soon brought a young lady to be introduced to Jamie. Tom listened shamelessly to the conversation, wanting to tease Jamie.

"Ah declare, you scouts must be the bravest of Marion's

Brigade," the young lady simpered. "Now that this terrible war is over, will you be going back to your plantation, Mr. McCaskill?"

"No, miss. I suspect there is a lot of war still to be fought. I'll stay with General Marion as long as he needs me."

"And do you have a wife waiting for you at home?"

"No," Jamie replied and, not liking the glint in the young woman's eye, he added, "I intend to take a wife as soon as this is over."

"From a plantation on the coast, I imagine. Or Charleston, perhaps."

"No. A girl from a farm in Camden has caught my eye," Jamie explained.

"Oh, a country girl. I suppose she shares your feelings on this war."

"Oh, yes, and she spied for Francis Marion. Once she rode two days through the swamp to warn the general of a plan to trap him. She's a brave lass."

"And big and strong, I imagine. Why, I couldn't begin to manage a horse for that distance. I'm too ladylike to do more than pour tea Papa says."

"Ann is smaller and slighter than you. It doesn't take brute strength to control a mount. You just have to be brighter than the horse."

Jamie caught Tom Bixby's eye and gave him a quick wink. He heard Tom chortle.

The young girl looked puzzled and started to take leave of him. Jamie bowed low as she moved off.

Tom moved closer. "Jamie, m'boy. I don't think she realized that your remark was very ungentlemanly. If you make a comment like that to Ann you best be prepared for her temper."

"That I know, Tom. That I know. I remember a few times when Ann has let me know of her displeasure. First time was when Ben and I found her in the swamp. I still thought she was a child of 8 or 9, and told her she couldn't keep up with us so one would ride slower with her. She let me know she was no child and she was as fine a rider as many who rode with Marion. And she was not shy about telling me. But usually, she is shy. It's hard to know what she is thinking."

"Can't say I am any more enlightened than you. I do know she thinks a plantation owner is far above her station."

"Not so, Tom. Not so."

"Jamie, Ann was just a child when this struggle began and I enlisted in the South Carolina regiment. I've missed so much of my children's life and it will take time to know them again. I knew that Jack passed information about Camden to you but I never realized how deeply involved Ann was. It was a great shock to see her at Snows Island. I never imagined that she harbored such patriot feelings."

"She's a brave lass, Tom," Jamie observed.

"Yes, but that young lady who just left us would think Ann unpolished and countrified and Ann would agree. Plantation life on the coast may be very different than Ann is accustomed to at Jack's farm."

"Ay, yes. The landed gentry," Jamie remarked caustically. "I well know that the coastal society believes itself superior, but I know different. A neighbor had hopes of me marrying his daughter and thus securing a good position for her. She was much like the young lady we just spoke to, a simpering, decorative piece. I had no interest in her and my parents agreed that she was not suitable. When this trouble started, that family plotted with the British to get our land by accusing my father. They informed on him and he was hanged. Other neighbors were Tory and I have only contempt for them. If they survive this struggle I shall certainly not court their daughters."

"Their loss, Jamie. You're a fine man," Tom complimented.

"When this is over, we will need to rebuild. I want a wife I can trust to help with the rebuilding. Not a decorative piece for the living room. Make no mistake, Tom Bixby. I intend to court your daughter."

Tom put his arm around Jamie's shoulders. "And you'll be welcome, boy."

Tom looked over the celebrating guests one last time. "I think I'll go back to my bed. Without my family here these festivities don't interest me."

"Nor me, Tom," Jamie commented. "I'll pay my respects to the host and hostess. I can beg off since I have dispatches to write."

"Tonight?"

"No, not tonight, but they need not know that."

Tom and Jamie left the Cantey house and walked away towards their camp. It was a quiet night outside the lighted house but militia wandered about.

Oscar, Marion's slave, stood close to the house, rifle in hand, standing watch.

"All quiet?" Tom asked.

"Yessir," Oscar replied.

The men knew that in spite of the festivities, there was still danger. Cantey was widely known as a Whig and Marion's presence would surely be known in the area. It was not prudent to let one's guard down. The men who rode with Marion realized that the Swamp Fox was a target of any ambitious Tory who wished to make a name for himself and to curry favor with the British.

Cornwallis might be gone, but there were still many British troops in the Carolinas. How they would respond to Cornwallis' defeat was not yet known. This was no time to be lax.

Oscar was not the only partisan who watched Marion closely. Others were near by. As long as Marion was a threat to the British and Tories, he'd be a target. His men had no intention of letting an enemy near.

Tom and Jamie nodded to the men who stood guarding the house and yard, and knew there would be others picketed down the approaches to the Cantey place. They could sleep well tonight.

As they walked on, a sudden thought struck Tom.

"Jamie, does your mother know of your plans?"

"Absolutely."

"And does she approve?"

"She does. Heartily. Her only concern is that our properties are so far apart and, with Ann so young, she might miss her family."

"Yes, I can see that. But yet again, Ann has had to grow up rapidly in these times. When our last baby was born and didn't live long, Ann had to take over the household as my gentle Nell was so sick. We almost lost her, too. But Ann took care of her mother and Tad when Jack and I left to join the South Carolina Regiment. She's seen the badly wounded from battle and has been forced to watch men hanged. She's been a great comfort to Jack. And her spying was not a game for children. She's old for her young years."

"That she is, and I hope that travel will be less perilous in the future so we can be in communication."

Tom was quiet for a moment. "Jack had always wanted us to move to the farm but I wanted to make my own way. Didn't want to be the younger brother taking orders. It would have been easier for Nell had I listened to Jack and settled my family at the farm. Now, I surely will settle there as Jack needs us."

"Ann and Tad both love the farm and that gives me hope that she will be happy at our plantation. But first, I have to court her. She may have other ideas. Like Robbie Stuart."

"Not in this life, friend. Not Ann and that pretend patriot," Tom laughed at the thought.

"But it is not yet the time to think of such things," Jamie remarked. "The surrender of Cornwallis is a great blow for the British Army, but there are many more of the enemy here. General Clinton has a huge army in New England, and we have troops in Charleston who still can do much mischief."

"I'm more worried about the Tory militia," Tom confessed.

135

"They are paid by the British but they are motivated by hate. Will they retreat to Charleston with the rest or will they stay closer to their homes and continue to fight? Possibly there is still much bloodshed ahead."

"And it's not only the Tories," Jamie commented soberly. "The Whigs, who have suffered much, will take vengeance on their enemies when the British can no longer protect them. Already we've had hangings enough in the Camden area since the British left there. I fear there are many months of turmoil ahead."

"Perhaps the next reports from General Greene will give us some idea of what we have ahead. Sleep well, Jamie," Tom advised.

"Good night."

The orders from Greene meant no more rest for the brigade. They moved out and patrolled the low country keeping the British from venturing too far from Charleston. But there were few encounters with the enemy as Marion had no ammunition. It was just a game of watching and waiting as the patriot noose move tighter and tighter around Charleston Neck. But the great danger to the state came, not from the British in Charleston, but from the Tories in the upcountry. The head of the serpent had been cut off with the defeat of Cornwallis but the tail of the serpent still thrashed in the Carolinas.

Sixteen

Bixby Farm

"Ann! Ann!" an excited Tad shouted, racing into the garden where Ann was picking fresh green collards.

"What is it, Tad?" a curious Ann replied.

"Papa's home! Papa's home!"

"Where is he?" Ann grabbed her basket and hurried towards the house.

"In the kitchen, with Mum and Aunt Raye."

Ann quickly climbed the steps to the porch and entered the house. She moved down the hall and across the keeping room to the back door and out into the yard between the house and the outside kitchen.

Tom Bixby braced himself as his two children launched themselves into his arms.

"Papa! Is the war over?" an excited Tad asked. "Are you home for always?"

Ann wondered at that. She knew of the British defeat at Yorktown and wondered if her father was now safe.

"No, son. Not yet."

"But the British are beaten," Tad argued. "Can't you stop fighting now?"

"If only we could, son," Tom Bixby responded sadly. "If only we could."

Tom Bixby released his children and looked at Ann.

"You've grown, Wee Ann, since I was last here. Or should I call you Sweet Ann as Jamie does?"

Ann blushed.

"Did you come alone, Papa?"

"Yes, Ann. The general had things to arrange for the governor. He sent me to see to things in Camden and Jamie and other milita went into the PeeDee to monitor things there."

Jack Bixby joined the group and thumped Tom on the back with his one good hand.

"Trouble, Tom?" Jack asked. "I've heard things are heating up with the Tories."

"Exactly. When Camden was first evacuated and all the troublesome Tories departed with them, this was a relatively safe place. Safe enough for General Greene's wife to visit and for Governor Rutledge to use the area for his headquarters. Now the governor plans to move his operations closer to Greene's area of protection and the general is ordered to help. But Tories are gathering strength behind the lines and that is a worry."

"I heard in Camden that Cunningham is campaigning again," Jack commented.

"That he is," Tom answered, "and that is why I'm here. Tomorrow we need to visit the local farms and warn them of Bloody Bill's tactics. He can't be trusted and he's a violent and brutal animal."

"So I hear," Jack agreed. "Is he still west of the Edisto?"

"Seems so, but with several hundred Tories encamped along the Edisto, he has many reinforcements. Had about 300 with him when they attacked patriots at Clouds Creek between the Edisto and the Little Saluda River."

"Many casualties?" Jack inquired.

"The patriot force was about thirty. Two escaped. The rest were slaughtered. Two days later he attacked patriots at Col.

Hayes home. When Cunningham threatened to burn his house down around his family, Hayes surrendered. As he walked out with his good wife, he was shot dead on the spot. Cunningham personally killed him and then the rest of the captured men. The Tories plundered the home and then fled."

"What does he hope to gain?" Jack asked.

"Hard tellin'. But we need to be prepared if he comes this way. Every farm needs to be warned and ready. There is no surrender to that savage."

"Why didn't Jamie and Ben accompany you?" Raye asked.

"There may be trouble in the PeeDee. We had a truce with the Tories there. The governor offered to let them keep their lands if they swore loyalty to the cause and served six months in the militia. The offer was accepted, but another notorious Tory commander, David Fanning, has moved out of North Carolina and into the Cheraw area and west. If he recruits those former Tories, we could have more blood shed in the PeeDee. Fanning is another ruthless Tory commander although I think he's less bloodthirsty than Bloody Bill Cunningham. In any case, we best be prepared."

After the supper meal, plans were made for the following morning.

"What do you need from me, Tom?" a curious Jack asked.

"I think we should make the rounds of the local farms and prepare them for the worst. They need to know that they cannot surrender to Cunningham without losing their lives. I'd like Ezra and Noah to ride with me and armed."

"I'll have them get the long rifles in the morning," Jack replied.

"No, not those. Armed slaves are a threat to many of the neighbors. It would be best if they carried fowling pieces loaded with goose shot. I'd like our neighbors to realize how much protection they would have if they armed their households. That goose shot could do a lot of damage even in the hands of a woman."

"I don't think most of the men would relish their women-folk fighting. Perhaps they could help somehow, but fire a weapon?" Jack wondered.

"But we all could fight," a worried Ann spoke. "We have practiced with our weapons and Mom, Aunt Raye and I all are tolerable shots."

"Better than tolerable," Jack agreed.

"And the young slaves can reload right and rapid and give the men more fire power," Ann insisted.

Tom reached to hug his daughter to him. "I know, Ann, Jack has trained his household well but most do not understand the brutality of this war. They think their womenfolk are safe from violence and they are not. It is too much to hope that they would arm their women and teach them to protect themselves, but perhaps we could get them to arm their slaves with fowling pieces. It won't be easy. I hear Robbie Stuart was appalled that Ben was so well armed."

"Oh, Robbie Stuart," an exasperated Ann fussed.

"He's sweet on Ann," Tad teased.

"Hush, Tad," Ann admonished. "I'm surely not sweet on him."

Tom smiled. He was glad to hear that and he knew of another who would be similarly relieved.

Jack had been quiet for a moment. Now he spoke.

"The field work is done and I can spare the workers to ride patrol in the area, especially at night. We'd have to be careful about it. No use in the whole area knowing what kind of fire power we have here."

"I've been thinking we should urge the neighbors to mount patrols of their own. If Cunningham crosses the Edisto and starts for the Wateree, we should have some warning. But in case the scouts fail, we should have our own patrols in place," Tom decided.

"How much should we tell the neighbors?" Jack wondered aloud.

"We should acquaint them with Col. Haye's fate. If they

think there is any mercy in Cunningham, they should think again. If we work together, we can surely lessen the threat that Bloody Bill poses."

"What about the Stuarts? If they really are Tory, as Ann suspects, could we trust them?" Nell Bixby wondered aloud.

"Robbie Stuart rides with a unit of Thomas Sumter's militia. His family would be a target of the Tories no matter what their feelings on the matter. I think we need to drive that home to Mrs. Stuart as well as her husband."

"Let me ride with you, Papa," Ann pleaded. "I'll be sure the women understand that their husbands will be killed in front of them if they don't resist."

"What is this world coming to?" a distraught Nell Bixby asked. "I hate the thought of all this."

"She'll be safe, Nell," Tom promised. "I will not risk Ann, but she is right. The men won't talk of atrocities to their womenfolk. Ann could certainly make the danger clear over a cup of tea."

It was decided.

The next few days, Tom, Jack, Ezra and Noah rode to the surrounding neighbors and Ann accompanied them. At every household she was invited to visit with the women of the house while the men talked of war.

Ann spent her time with the women profitably.

"You can't mean it, Ann" a distraught Mrs. Stuart exclaimed as she pushed another scone towards Ann.

"I certainly do, Mrs. Stuart," Ann replied. "In every case, Cunningham has killed the men who surrendered and at Hayes' home, Mrs. Hayes was at her husband's side when Cunningham struck him down."

"What is this world coming to?" Mrs. Stuart asked no one in particular.

"I believe that we will all be safe if everyone watches for Cunningham and bands together to oppose him if he crosses the Wateree. He would surely burn and pillage one farm at a time if he were unopposed. Of course, we are targets, but so are the Stuarts, since Robbie rides with Sumter."

The enormity of the situation was reflected on Mrs. Stuart's face.

Poor lady, Ann thought. This is probably the first time Mrs. Stuart had considered the danger they were all in.

"I thought this conflict would end when the British evacuated Camden, but still the danger continues," the worried mother commented. "And so close to Christmas."

Ann had no patience for Robbie Stuart but she understood his mother's pain.

Ann explained how vigilance would protect them all and then the matter was dropped.

She wondered if Mrs. Stuart knew that Robbie had expressed interest in her but didn't know how to broach the subject. She didn't need to.

"I see that your Uncle Jack is riding with your father. I thought he was too poorly to get around," Mrs. Stuart observed.

"He's improved considerably in the last few months," Ann reported. No need to mention his pretense at being an invalid when there was that need.

"I thought he would never be able to manage his farm again and that work is just too much for poor Rachel," Mrs. Stuart continued.

Poor Rachel, indeed, Ann thought. Her Aunt Raye was the strongest and most capable woman one could imagine. Certainly able to run the farm if necessary. Far more capable than many of the men in the area.

"Uncle Jack is now able to manage things and, when this terrible conflict is over, my papa will help."

"Oh, your mother and father will not return to Camden?"

"No. With no children of their own, Uncle Jack and Aunt Raye want us to stay. Tad is already a great help and will soon take his place in the operation of the farm."

"And will you be happy with that, Ann?"

"Oh, yes. I love my aunt and uncle and the farm is home

now."

Ann hoped that the Stuarts understood that the men of the family would manage the farm. She'd suspected that Robbie was more interested in Jack's farm than in courting her. With her father and Tad at the farm, there was no need of Robbie Stuart's help!

Ann took leave of Mrs. Stuart after thanking her for the lovely scones.

After supper the Bixby family talked of the day's activities.

"Do you think our neighbors are fully aware of the danger, Tom?" Raye asked.

"Believe so," Tom replied. "We certainly let them know how dangerous a Tory attack would be."

"Will they be ready to fight, if necessary?" Nell asked.

"Probably. They do know we have to unite if Cunningham comes to the Wateree. We've promised to provide help but they must keep watch and warn us."

"Yes," agreed Jack. "We are the farthest from danger here at the edge of the swamp and, if they want help, they need to warn us in time. Seems most are willing to put out patrols but we will mount our own. I've already alerted Ezra and Noah to rotate the duties and be sure that we have men out every night. Want them close to the edge of our property and checking on any strangers."

"Yes," said Tom, "we don't want to be surprised."

"If Cunningham should invade with significant numbers we might have to flee to the swamp. We'll go over our escape plans again tomorrow. I want to be sure every living soul on this farm knows how to move through the swamp to safety."

The next few days were exciting for Tad and the young boys on the farm. If retreat from the farm was necessary, Tad would be in charge of moving the horses across the wet area behind the house to the hammock, the firm little island, just beyond. The path from behind the stables, down the bluff to the safe passage, was steep and the horses would have to be led.

"Hold tight to the lead, Tad," his father called. "Just walk him down the path."

"Couldn't we ride them down the trail behind the house like you, Jamie and Ben do?"

"No, son," Tom replied. "Uncle Jack is directing a tree to be felled and propped over that incline. If we have to flee, the tree will be pushed over to keep horsemen from riding down to the bottomland below. If a rider tried to jump the tree he'd find himself in mid air."

Tad smiled at the thought. Flying Tories!

"We'll bring our horses down here and get them over to the other side of the marshy area here. We can withdraw and keep any riders from following us. Once we are all across this marsh and into the swamp we'll not be followed. A Tory try-ing to negotiate this terrain would be a fine target. Besides, there is not a man in the area who does not believe this swamp to be inpenetrable. Even the locals would think we would be hopelessly lost in there, and the swamp along the Black River is even more threatening. No, son. Once we have the house-hold down the bluff and into the swamp we are safe."

Tad took to his task with greater enthusiasm. The women arranged some foodstuffs in packets to fit into saddlebags and stored them, along with food in barrels, in the caves in the bluff.

Every day which passed without incident relieved the hearts of the adults, while Tad and his young "recruits" planned great escapades. Even knowing the seriousness of the threat, the young anticipated great excitement.

As Christmas day approached the threat of an attack seemed less likely.

"Should we try to attend a church meeting in Camden?" Nell Bixby asked while the adults sat around the table in the keeping room.

"I'd rather not, Nell," Tom Bixby replied. "It is too far to ride when danger still lurks."

"But we haven't heard any more about Cunningham," Ann offered.

"No, nor Fanning. We've had no word from Jamie about what is happening along the Waccamaw and PeeDee. I'd rather we spend the day here in prayer and song. And pray fervently that next Christmas will find us all free."

A yule log was lighted and the work should have stopped for all the farm, but Tad still drilled his little platoon every day.

"That boy can't get his mind from the war." Jack observed. "Just like us, I suppose."

"We were once that excited, and thought it would be a great adventure," Tom reflected, "but I'm sick of war. I count the days when the excitement is passed and things are quiet again."

"I'll say 'Amen' to that," Jack added quietly.

Seventeen

Bixby Farm

It had been a quiet Christmas, Ann thought. There had been no news of Tory attacks. Perhaps the war would be over soon and Papa could come home to stay.

The day was warm for the last of December. One of those sunny Carolina days when just a gentle breeze stirred the air. Ann had shaken out the bedding and put it on the porch railings to freshen. She was straightening a corner when she heard the call from the swamp.

The cries of the crows had not immediately caught her attention, but suddenly she was aware of the pattern.

Two caws—one—then three— then one, and a final two.

It had been some months since that code had been signaled to the household that all was well with Marion's scouts. Jamie and the Bixby household had used that signal many times before and there was no doubt in Ann's mind who the caller was now.

She left the porch and walked to the edge of the bluff as Jamie's horse struggled to the top of the incline. Ben was still on the flat swampy area below, leading two heavily laden mules.

"You didn't answer the signal, Ann," Jamie laughed.

"You gave me little enough time for that before I heard the horse on the path," Ann replied.

"Well, we did a bit of scouting and knew that all was well here before we signaled. Just wanted to remind you of the old days," Jamie admitted.

"I haven't forgotten," Ann told him.

No, she hadn't forgotten anything about Jamie McCaskill!

"Ann, Ben needs some help getting those mules to move up. Is Ezra here?"

"No, he rode to Camden with Papa, Uncle Jack and Tad," Ann explained. "But Noah was at the smith. Could I help?"

"'Fraid not, Wee Ann. Those mules are heavily packed and they will need a lot of persuadin' to get up that steep path."

He looked at the hewn tree propped to the side of the path at the top of the bluff.

"Looks like you were expecting trouble."

"Uncle Jack thought it would discourage any riders from plunging down the bluff if we had to take to the swamp. Fortunately it was not necessary."

"Fortunately," Jamie echoed.

"What is on the mules?" Ann wondered aloud.

"Sacks of rice from our plantation. We've not been plundered as extensively as some and the yield was heavy. Best rice in the Carolinas," Jamie boasted. "And salt, and some herbs Maudie sent for Hattie. And some Peruvian bark to replace the cure you gave me when I had camp fever. Jack gave me the last you had on this farm even knowing he couldn't replace it except from Charleston. And that was unlikely. My mother had a supply so I've brought some. And. . ."

Jamie hesitated.

"And?" Ann queried.

"And a few surprises," Jamie teased.

With Noah's help the mules were brought to the outdoor kitchen and the sacks of rice unloaded and stacked as Hattie

147

directed. Salt was carefully stored as it was like gold, needed to preserve their meat.

"What's going on in Camden that the Bixbys are there?"

"Not too much, I hope. There has been no news of Cunningham's Tories lately and Papa wanted to see what the word in Camden is. Tad rode with them and he was much excited to be included. They expect no trouble."

"Glad to hear it," Jamie exclaimed.

"And your home, Jamie?" Ann asked. "Is your mother well and the area safe?"

"I 'spect so. We'd expected some trouble but none developed. Several of the militia accompanied me and their presence might have made the Tories cautious. It was a quiet Christmas for which we were thankful. And mother is very well and sends her regards to you and your family."

It was close to supper time when the Bixbys returned from Camden.

"I'm ready for a good meal, Nell," Tom Bixby announced. "Nothing like a long ride to whet an appetite."

"That's a fact," Tad added, importantly.

Jamie distributed gifts he had brought to the family and Tad was excited to see the wooden games Jamie had brought from his home. Not new games, but games Jamie had as a child. Ann was touched by his generosity.

"And for you, Sweet Ann," Jamie teased as he handed her an exquisitely crafted wooden box.

Ann turned the lovely little box over in her hands and marveled at the smooth inlay.

"It's lovely, Jamie," Ann said quietly. "Thank you."

"But you must open it, Ann," Jamie insisted. "The real gift is inside."

Ann carefully opened the little box and peered inside. She lifted the contents: a large silver ring hung on a beautiful silver chain.

"It's a watch, Ann," Jamie explained. "They call it a

shepherd's watch. Come out in the sun and I'll show you how it works."

The pair walked off the porch toward the garden.

"You move the two rings so the present month is beside the notch. Then you hold up the watch and a point of sun light will come through that little hole and strike one of the numbers on the ring. That tells you the hour."

"Oh, Jamie. It is lovely. I'll treasure it always."

She started to put the watch back in the box but Jamie stopped her. He took the chain and lifted it over her head and eased it around her neck.

"I want you to wear it, Ann. And whenever you lift it to the sun, say a prayer for me."

"You are always in my prayers, Jamie. You and Papa and General Marion and Ben and Oscar. Always."

That would have to do for now, Jamie thought. He dared not say too much. There was still a dangerous time ahead.

After supper the family and their guest sat in the keeping room where a small fire burned brightly keeping off the evening chill.

"What news from Camden?" Jamie asked.

"Nothing new there," Jack replied. "We'd worried about Cunningham but it seems Sumter's men are between the Wateree and the Edisto. I think we can leave Bloody Bill to them."

"Then we're safe here, Uncle Jack?" a curious Tad wondered. "Then Papa and Jamie won't have to fight any more."

"Yes, Tad, I believe we're safe here but Papa and Jamie still have things to take care of."

Tad looked puzzled.

Tom Bixby drew on his pipe as he looked at the anxious faces around the room.

"Things are not settled yet, Son," Tom began. "The British lost Cornwallis' army at Yorktown but there are other armies in the country. Word has it that England wants to quit the fight but that may take months to accomplish. In the meantime, we have to take as much land from the British as possible.

"In Europe, where the British usually fight, the treaties give each country the land they occupy when the fighting stops. If that should be the case here, the British would get most of our ports like Charleston, New York, Savannah and Wilmington, while we are left with small towns on the coast like Georgetown. They would control our shipping and we'd be more like losers than winners."

"But George Washington wouldn't let them do that, would he?" Tad worried.

"No, the Americans wouldn't like that at all, but we have French allies who will also be involved. They have other worries in the Caribbean and Europe and may want a quick peace."

"Yes, " added Jamie, "and that's why we have to push the British out of our territory now."

"How much territory do they hold?" Raye asked.

"Mostly Charleston Neck, and they venture out to get beeves and other supplies. We have to keep them contained and discourage the Tories from providing them aid and comfort."

"And what about Tories like Fanning and Cunningham?" Nell wondered.

"Governor Rutledge wants us to round up the families that the Tories left at home and take them to Charleston and hand them over to the British. That will lessen the threat in the back country and will increase the demands on the British to provide food and shelter. The British used the Tories to fight the war and to harass Whigs and patriots. Rutledge says, let the traitors look to their masters for their keeping."

"All the Tories?" Nell asked.

"No. There are hopes that many will see the error of their ways and pledge their allegiance to the state and join our militia. After this war is over and the British are gone, we will have to rebuild and bitterness and retribution will impede the process," Tom explained.

"So the fighting is over?" a hopeful Tad asked.

"No, Son," Tom answered. "Not yet. There will be resistance to the governor's plan and some might be violent but let us pray that the worst is over."

"So you and Jamie will fight to push back the British," Nell commented.

"No, Mrs. Bixby," Jamie answered. "Tom will take care of brigade business but I will be with General Marion. The governor has decided to manage the affairs of the state from Jacksonboro, down on the Edisto, close to Charleston. Marion was elected as one of the members of the assembly and I'll accompany him. Both the governor and Greene write voluminous reports to which they expect replies. Marion is a man of action, not a man of letters, so I will take care of those reports."

Tom said nothing but he knew it was not a safe position. Marion and Greene were to protect the assembly but the Continental Congress had not provided enough supplies or ammunition to do the job properly. It will be the same old situation, Tom thought. Too many demands and too few resources. Jacksonboro was little more than thirty miles from Charleston and British mounted troops could cover that distance in a day. There would be encounters and more blood shed, but there was no need to discomfort the ladies.

"When will you have to leave, Papa?" a worried Ann asked.

"Tomorrow, at first light. Jamie?"

"Certainly. Marion has been in the low country for the last few weeks and I expect the sooner Ben and I get there, the better."

"Ben will accompany you?" Ann asked.

"Yes. Marion trusts us to be vigilant as to his safety. For all his huge size, Ben moves quietly about and hears much of value to us. And I feel more secure under his protection than the Continentals that Greene provides. Ben will know that Edisto swamp in a day and that will be a great help. Of course, we were at Parker's Ferry so know the road system and the ferries. But Ben will reconnoiter and we'll have excellent intelligence. There's not a finer scout in the brigade, and Marion has great faith in him."

"Will Oscar scout, too?" an inquisitive Tad asked.

"No. Oscar will attend Marion. They have campaigned together since the beginning and Oscar can anticipate Marion's every need. He also knows the danger Marion poses to the British and Tories and how badly they'd like to dispose of him. Oscar is exceedingly watchful and cautious. And in that group of representatives, few will notice slaves who hover in the background."

Jack Bixby rose from his chair. "It was a tiring ride today and I'll be up to see you off in the morning. Will someone see to the fire?"

"I'll do it, Jack," Jamie offered. "I should check with Ben about tomorrow."

"Can I come, Jamie?" Tad asked.

Jamie looked at Tad's mother who nodded her agreement.

"Certainly. And Ann, will you walk with us?"

Ann took her cloak from the peg on the wall and moved toward the door.

On the porch, Tad moved to take Jamie's hand. Ann reached to take Tad's other hand but Jamie took her hand in his and pulled the two along toward the outside kitchen.

They found Ben and Hattie engaged in conversation about the herbs Maudie had sent. Some of the herbs had been dried but others, found only in the coastal swamps, were rooted and wrapped in wet Spanish moss and dirt. Ben was giving directions about their care and their use.

"We will leave at first light, Ben," Jamie announced.

"The hosses will be ready," Ben answered as he smiled and nodded to Ann and Tad as they left the cabin.

"Look at the stars, Jamie," Tad demanded. "And the moon. It's so clear tonight it must mean a good day for tomorrow."

"Hope so. I don't mind the rain in season but it can make

it hard going when it's this time of year," Jamie replied.

Ann was silent as the three stood watching the starry sky.

Suddenly Tad broke the silence. "Jamie, we didn't get to sing your lassie song!"

"That's right. Let's sing it now and sing it with a fast meter as we need to move smartly. We've been standing too long in this cold."

Jamie started the verse and Ann and Tad joined in as the three marched briskly across the Bixby yard toward the house. Jamie sang, in a clear voice, the words he'd reflected on so often:

Will you go, lassie, go?
And we'll all go together
Over wild mountain thyme
And the blooming heather.
Will you go, lassie, go?
He looked at Ann and again wondered.
Will you go, lassie, go?

The household rose early and ate with the departing patriots. Ben brought the horses round and Tom and Jamie walked out on the porch. Along the edge of the swamp the fog was thick and a light mist hung over the fields.

"Will clear to a fine day, I 'spect," Tom Bixby decided. He reached to give his wife and children a last embrace.

Ann turned to Jamie. She reached to the silver watch on the chain round her neck.

"Thank you, Jamie. Your gift is most generous." Far too generous, Ann thought.

"You are most welcome, Ann. Our family is beholden to you for your care of Ben and me. We might easily have perished but for Jack's concern and Hattie's care. This farm has been a refuge for us and it's grateful the McCaskills are."

He mounted his horse and sat looking down at Ann's flushed face. He was pleased that she liked the gift and wondered what she might think of the other package he had carried and which Ann's mother had hidden away for later. Not too much later, he hoped.

The Legislature

Jamie and Ben arrived at Jacksonboro as the members of the new legislature were assembling. It had been the brigade's task to secure the area and to be sure the members had safe conduct. Greene was confident that the British from Charleston could be contained, but the Tories were another matter.

"I'm glad you're here, Jamie," Marion remarked when Jamie reported to him.

"Glad to be here, Senator," Jamie addressed his leader with the new title.

"Would have been happier to stay with the brigade," Marion confessed. "Here I am harassed on every side. Greene wants my attention for warfare and the governor has other ideas."

"Anything I can help with, Sir?" Jamie offered.

"I'd be obliged if you'd be my eyes and ears. The governor's first concern is to stop the bloodshed between the Patriots and the Tories. The brigade has fallen off, first from lack of ammunition and then, from squabbling among the leaders. Greene has taken much of the command to form cavalry and that has caused great friction. And my most trusted men have homes far from Charleston and they aren't happy to be at such great distance from their families. It has been a long and troubled time and the men and their horses are wore out."

Jamie nodded in agreement.

"But your family, Jamie? Is your mother well? And what is the situation in the PeeDee?"

"All is quiet. No Tory action to speak of. And Mother is well. Of course, she is eager for this war to be over, but she has managed to keep the plantation running and intact, for the most part. Most of the raiding was done when the British first arrived in the area. Now that they have been pushed back, the Tories are not so bold."

"And the Bixbys? I understand you stop with Tom's family as you pass through that area."

"They are well, Sir. I owe a great debt to that family. They cared for Ben when I despaired of him recovering from such a wound. And they cared for me when I was too ill to care for myself."

"Yes, Jamie. They are fine people. But I understand from Tom that you have a special interest in one family member."

Jamie blinked at the uncharacteristic remark. Francis Marion was not one for trivial conversation.

"Yes, I care very much for Tom's daughter, Ann."

"A good choice, my boy. She is a brave girl and loyal when others faltered in their devotion to independence. It's a fine family and you could choose no better."

During the next few days Jamie saw many familiar faces among the members of the legislature. The people had great confidence in their partisan leaders and they were there. Thomas Sumter was a senator, as was Marion, and Andrew Pickens was a representative.

Jamie watched as the senators worked. They had great responsibility but there was much confusion. The governor wanted the war over and the bloodshed among the South Carolinians to cease. But he also wanted the Tories to suffer for, what he termed, treasonous behavior. The task of the senate was not an easy one.

Jamie especially watched Thomas Sumter and Francis Marion. The two great leaders were intent on making the state safe and they worked to that purpose. That was not really surprising. Marion, although not a social person, and the affable Sumter had been acquainted since long before the war and had many friends in common.

Sumter was popular with the legislature. He was a handsome man of great poise and charm. He was well-respected for his intellect and his soldiering. But it was the soldiering which stuck in Jamie's craw.

For as a military commander, Sumter was brash and impatient. Sumter would, Jamie knew, always consider the battle at Quinby Bridge one of his great victories. He had inflicted heavy casualties on the British who had neither the time or the means to replace the dead soldiers. He had inflicted wounds which would strain the medical facilities of the British. He had forced the British unit to abandon their position at Monck's Corner and to move back to Charleston. Yes, the goal had been achieved.

But Marion would look at things differently. He would mourn the loss of so many good men; men who had been with him through perilous times and who had depended on him to shed their blood dearly. Jamie thought of the men they had buried in a common grave in that sodden, sweltering, stinking swamp. He thanked a merciful God that he and Ben had not been among those unfortunate patriots. Yes, Marion would forever count the cost while Sumter would focus on the gain.

It was a difference in the military perspective.. Marion was rare among commanders in his concern for his men, Jamie thought. He was glad that he took his orders from the cantankerous, but compassionate, little Swamp Fox.

157

Jamie shared Marion's concern over the break-up of the brigade. Greene sent detachments of Marion's men to secure the area, to accompany families of Tories to Charleston, and to fill the ranks of the two troops of cavalry he had established.

Marion was eager to get back and reestablish his command but the governor forbade it. Without Marion there would not be quorum, or sufficient number of legislators, to conduct the state's business. Jamie and Marion both chafed under the yoke of government.

In February Marion had been able to quit Jacksonboro and had met British cavalry at Wambaw Creek. Many of the "six month men", former Tories, deserted the field leaving the remainder of the brigade vulnerable. Marion had been forced to retreat from the field in good order. But "in good order" was not to Marion's liking and he yearned to settle the account.

It was August before he got another chance.

As part of the brigade assembled at Fair Lawn, Jamie was able to express his fears to Tom Bixby.

"It's not my way of fightin', Tom," Jamie admitted. "We have only the officers and a few scouts mounted. Those cavalry units are a poor excuse for the kind of mounted we fielded in the old days. Those commanders have no sense of loyalty to Marion and seem determined to thwart his authority."

"Seems so," a tired Tom Bixby replied. "I keep hopin' the action will soon be over. The politicians are in Paris trying to end the war but they move slow. Every encounter here means more dead, friends or enemies."

"I don't think men matter much to people who are not at risk. What do you know of this operation?"

"Fraser is back plunderin'. Guess he didn't get enough ball and buckshot at Parker's Ferry," Tom observed.

"Fraser is a Tory from New Jersey, and the men he commands are South Carolinians. I just can't figger why he persists, when the British parliament has given up the struggle.

Why does this madness continue?"

"Hard tellin'," Tom replied. "Hard tellin'. I suspect Fraser is rounding up cattle for Charleston, but he'll attack if he gets the chance."

And Tom Bixby was right. Fraser's troopers approached Fair Lawn and Marion sent his mounted officers to scout the approach. The cavalry which was to support Marion was miles away. The brigade sought the shelter of the thick cedars and waited for the attack.

Fraser's mounted were within thirty yards of the cedars when the brigade fired a volley of buckshot. Men and horses went down under the barrage. Victory seemed certain.

But the blast of the volley panicked the horses harnessed to Marion's ammunition wagons and they stampeded away from the battle. With the reserve shot and powder gone, and no cavalry to retrieve the wagons, Marion ordered a retreat.

The brigade stayed in the field and on the move. Marion became increasingly impatient as the talks in Paris dragged on. News from Europe was slow, but the British had already evacuated Wilmington and Savannah. It was just a matter of time before they left Charleston. But the evacuation would be cumbersome. There were thousands of Tories and even more slaves to be transported out of the Carolinas, and the sooner the better, Jamie thought.

Finally word came that the departure date for the British would be December 14! Charleston was planning a great day for the departure of the British and the return of the Continental troops to establish American control. However, no militia would be there to participate or even to witness the event. Only the Continental Army and prominent citizens would participate in a great procession.

Jamie thought of the irony. A victory parade without the victors! Was the slight to the militia an intentional snub? Most

159

of the soldiers he had fought with knew the value of Marion's brigade. Would Generals Wayne and Greene have deliberately excluded these ragged men? The Continental soldiers were as ragged and unkempt as they.

No, Jamie thought, it was the Council of Charleston who didn't want the militia in their midst. It would be a reminder that while their people were wining and dining the British officers, their countrymen from the Carolina swamps, the river systems and the hills had saved the nation. Jamie smiled at the thought.

Rumor was that the militia was too undisciplined and might initiate a disturbance. Jamie remembered it was not the militia who had cost them the victory at Eutaw Springs. It was Continentals who stopped to loot the British camp and had turned a certain victory into a bloody defeat. No, Marion's brigade was disciplined enough.

But these men would not be welcome in the kitchens of Charleston let alone in the parlor for tea! But one would think the citizens of Charleston would be grateful to these men who had risked everything, lost everything and suffered for two and a half years.

But it seemed that was not likely. Perhaps that was the nature of war: The soldiers did the fighting and the generals took the credit. He remembered the scene that would be etched in his memory as long as he lived: dead soldiers impaled on each other's bayonets on the field at Eutaw Springs. Did either nation value the sacrifice of these common soldiers? Probably not. Certainly not the Council of Charleston.

But General Greene knew the value of Marion's campaign and had asked the Swamp Fox to accompany him to Charleston as his guest. Marion had refused. Made the excuse that he'd heard there was the smallpox in the city and, since he himself had not had the illness, he was reluctant to enter. No, Jamie thought, Marion would not take the honors his men were denied.

Jamie shook those thoughts from his head and turned

his attention to General Francis Marion's address to the troops. This was the final muster, a dismissal. Then, they would all depart from Fair Lawn.

He heard Marion thank the troops for what he termed the greatest hardship and fatigue with spirit and bravery which reflected the highest honor on them. He asserted that no citizens in the world had ever done more.

Marion concluded: "I cannot doubt in the least your readiness to turn out should this country be ever again so unhappy as to be invaded by her cruel and barbarous enemies. I wish you a long continuance of happiness and the blessings of peace."

Marion walked to where Oscar waited with the horses. He mounted, turned his back on Charleston, and headed home without another word.

The men stood quiet for a moment. There were tears on some faces. All were somber. It was not a moment of celebration but of completion. There were thoughts of the many men they had buried along the way and there were wounds that pained. Some were healed, others still raw. But it was over.

These were the men Marion had led into battle. Marion was a quiet men but he knew his brigade well. The conditions under which they had fought were beyond imagining. The hardships were more severe than any outsider could ever know. But Marion knew these men and he was right. Jamie looked at face after face and thought of the mettle of the men.

Now it was time to return to families and rebuild their homes. As if this was not quite real, men lingered. Some talked with comrades and then, in pairs and small groups, they departed. Some spoke to Jamie and Ben as they stood to the side. Others spoke briefly to Tom Bixby and some gave their captain a casual salute. It was over. Thank God, it was over!

These men were eager to see their loved ones again but Francis Marion was right. If ever their country needed them they would ride again. Jamie prayed that there would never be another time as perilous as these had been, but who knew what would come.

Jamie and Ben mounted as Tom Bixby rode to them. His face was tear stained, and it took a few minutes for him to regain his composure.

"Are you ready to ride to the PeeDee? Or can you spend a few days with us?" he asked.

Jamie did not hesitate. "Tom, thank you for your invitation. You know I will speak to Ann and, with your permission, make my feelings known. However, Ben and I will follow in a few days. We'll stop at Pond Bluff and offer what help we can to General Marion. I hear tell things are bad there and he can use some help. Now that he's no longer my commander, it will be easier to approach him and offer assistance. But have no fear, Tom, I'll be at the Bixby farm before long."

"Fine. I'll ride with you to the Santee and then ride along home."

The three mounted and rode away from the cedars at Fair Lawn.

Pond Bluff, Marion's home, was situated on a bluff overlooking the Santee. Being near the River Road, it had been plundered by foe and friend who passed the unprotected homestead in the last two and one half years. The buildings had been burned and anything of value which could be carried, had been carried off. Half of the slaves on the plantation had been taken, the others had fled into the swamp and survived there. Now that Francis Marion was back, they were coming out of hiding to join him.

The men worked to help clear the foundation until almost dark. They set up camp and ate a simple meal around the fire before they turned in for the night.

Early in the morning Tom Bixby left Jamie and Ben at Pond Bluff and headed for Nelson's Ferry, a short distance away.

After crossing the Santee, Tom set out north along the River Road to Camden. He galloped over the five bridges which spanned the swampy area along the river and thought of the battles they'd fought with Watson along that terrain.

He rode passed the lanes leading to Cantey's plantation and Thomas Sumter's plantation and did not hesitate. Another time he would stop and pay his respects, but not now.

At Scott's Lake he passed the deserted Fort Watson atop the Indian mound and remembered the days spent at that seige before the tower was built which assured their success. At Tarcote Swamp, just beyond, he shook his head at that debacle. The wild ride to cut off the retreating British that ended at Singleton's Mill and the shock of finding that family down with smallpox. It seemed then that even nature was against them.

As the road climbed away from swampy banks of the Wateree, Tom rode through the High Hills of the Santee, the "camp of ease" for the Continental Army. He stopped near the area where he had watched men digging graves on his last trip through this area. He dismounted and removed his hat.

As he stood there he thought of the many men who were buried in this place: men who had marched south with Greene's Continental Army with high hopes. Battles like Hopkirk Hill and Eutaw Springs had ended the lives of many of those brave men. Some were buried near where they fell, but others had been carried here and had died of wounds or disease.

Tom said a prayer for the men and for their families. He thanked God for his own survival and suddenly felt compelled to rush to his own family.

He had no interest in stopping at Camden so he skirted the area and headed for the Lynches River flood plain, the Bixby farm and his family. He hoped he would never have to leave again, certainly not under the circumstances of the past several years. He'd done what he felt he had to do, but he thanked God it was over.

Nineteen

Bixby Farm

It was a tired Tom Bixby who rode into the farm on that December afternoon. Nell embraced him warmly and he stood in the circle of his family and, for a long moment, he said nothing.

"It's over," he spoke quietly. "It's finally over. The British and their most obnoxious Tory friends are gone. It took 300 ships to evacuate them all but they are gone."

"Was there a great celebration in Charleston, Papa?" an excited Tad inquired.

"Perhaps, son," Tom replied. "But none of the militia were there to see it. The Council of Charleston wanted only the Continental Army. Those of us who fought so long and hard were considered too unruly to attend."

"That's not fair," an incensed Tad cried. "People should have cheered you and Jamie and Ben and General Marion."

"No matter, son," Tom assured him. "We were happier to get away from that swampy area and home to our families. All the cheers of Charleston are not worth one day's delay."

Ann approached her father and embraced him warmly. "I thank God that you are safely home. Are General Marion and Oscar well?"

"Yes, child. And Jamie and Ben, too."

"Have they gone back to the McCaskill plantation?"

"No, Ann. Jamie and Ben stopped at Pond Bluff, Marion's home. Jamie thought he and Ben might be of help so they were to stop there a few days. Jamie will stop here on his way to the PeeDee and his plantation."

Tom's first thought was for a good scrubbing and clean clothes. It was suppertime when the family assembled and talked of the future.

The next few days passed slowly for Ann in spite of the activity at the farm. Hattie prepared every favorite food for Tom and the spits were heavy with roasting meat.

When the next few days passed with no visitors, a dejected Ann concluded that Jamie had decided to bypass the Bixby's farm to go straight home. She walked briskly down to the creek bank and then slowly made her way to the small hammock in the swamp. It was here that she had so often met Jamie and delivered the intelligence she had gathered in Camden. She was glad the danger was over but she would miss the handsome scout.

Late in the afternoon a small body of horsemen approached; Ben was immediately recognized, then Jamie, but there were four Black men accompanying them. When they reached the outbuildings, Ben and the others took the horses and Jamie made his way to the porch. Nell Bixby embraced him warmly.

"My boy! How glad we are to see you safely through this terrible business! Come in! Come in!" She ushered him up to the porch where Raye embraced him.

A shy Ann stood back until Jamie spied her. "Come, Ann. Do you not wish to welcome me home?"

He saw the flushed cheeks and knew she was not comfortable with this, but he grabbed her and gave her a quick hug.

"Of course, Jamie," Ann sputtered. "We are glad to have you safe again."

"Ezra will see to Ben's needs and to that of the other men. Come and make yourself comfortable," Jack ordered.

"I am filthy from the swamp and the hard ride. I could use a washing if Hattie has her wash tubs ready. And again, could I borrow some clean clothes?"

Jack led Jamie off and Ann retreated to the kitchen to consult with the help about supper.

It was a clean Jamie McCaskill in borrowed Bixby clothing who greeted Ann in the keeping room. He stood close to the fire warming himself. The fit of Tom's clothes reminded Ann again that Jamie was no longer a boy. He was now a man of the same stature and size as her father and uncle.

"Such a luxury, Ann, to be warmed by a home fire. It has been a bit chilly although we spent many more uncomfortable nights in the campaign."

"How was General Marion?"

"He's well. His home is in a terrible state. The house was burned and everything of value was carried off, including some slaves. About ten were still living on the place and will help to rebuild. Ben and I and the men we've acquired helped clear the foundations and start the rebuilding. The general hopes to grow indigo and will need seed. I hope our plantation will be able to help provide some of those needs."

"Who are the men with Ben?" Ann asked.

"Escaped slaves who fought with Marion. They approached Ben about coming with us. They say they were owned by Tories who left with the British. I lost several slaves to the British and Tory looters and need more help. I'll need to supplement what we grow with game and these men are fine shots.

"And they can be trusted. That will be a great asset as I rebuild. Much of our stock is gone, and probably some seed which had not been hidden away. We are lucky that the buildings were left standing, but there is much to be done and extra hands will be useful. They are also fine horsemen and I hope to improve my stock."

"To race?"

"No. No. Some of my neighbors bred horses to race and sent the horses and slaves who cared for them to safer areas. Marion took all the horses he could from the Tories. We had to have the best horses in the state to move as we did. Tarleton confiscated all the horses he could find for the British troopers so there are few good horses left. And there are few breeders left as many were wealthy Tories and left with the British. I think I can breed good horses to sell but I'm not a gambler, Ann. I'll not race or wager on a race. I want to talk to Jack about breeding if he can give me the time."

"Won't your mother expect you to be at home?" a worried Ann asked.

"No, Ann. Mother knows I am safe and that I had business to attend to before I arrived in the PeeDee. I've sent word that I'll be along directly."

Supper was a quiet meal. There was just a little conversation about weather and some mention of the war. Food was plentiful and Jamie ate with great relish. He'd survived on limited rations for so long that every mouthful was enjoyed.

After the meal, the men moved to talk and the women settled themselves into the keeping room beside the fire. Ann could not help but wonder about Jamie's business which kept him away from his home.

Jamie approached the women where they sat and held out his hand to Ann.

"Will you walk with me, Ann?" he asked.

Ann nodded and moved to the wall where her hooded cape hung on a peg. Jamie took the cloak and wrapped it around her, then pulled the hood over her head. "It is a bit brisk outside but we'll not be long," he explained to Ann's mother.

The moonlight flooded the yard as they descended the step from the porch and walked to the edge of the bluff overlooking the creek where they had met so many times before. In the depths of the swamp it was dark and cold.

Jamie stopped at the edge of the bluff by a large oak with a low limb which hung close to the ground. He lifted Ann to sit on the limb and he leaned against it.

"Every visit after we chased the British south from Camden, I've known what I've wanted. Now that the time is here I have difficulty finding words to ask," Jamie confessed.

"Ask what, Jamie?" a puzzled Ann replied.

"Perhaps this should wait because you are so young. Yet the distance between here and my plantation is too far, and the work I have ahead too time consuming for me to leave often. I need you with me, Ann. I'm asking you to marry me. My sweet Ann, will you be my wife?"

A startled Ann stuttered a reply. "Yes. Oh, yes."

Jamie had planned on stealing a kiss or two but one look at Ann's face and he knew her kisses would be freely given and he lifted her down into his arms.

"It's too cold to linger here, Ann," Jamie declared. "It is best we go inside and speak to your family."

"They'll surely be surprised," Ann mused, as they walked, hand in hand, toward the house.

"Certainly not. For a long time I've talked with Tom and Jack about my intentions."

"How long?" Ann asked.

"I spoke to Tom after the surrender of Fort Motte. I knew when I left Camden after the evacuation that I would ask you to marry me when the danger was past. I would not have you pledged to me unless I survived whole from this bloody mess."

"But, Jamie, I would have cared for you if you were wounded," Ann protested.

"I knew that but some wounds were so horrible that men who survived threw themselves off the ferries returning them home. They would not face their families as useless men. They reasoned that it was better to leave wife and family free to find another husband rather than be saddled with a man who could not provide for the them."

"Jamie, you wouldn't . . ."

"No, but I had Ben and other slaves to care for me if I'd been a cripple, but I would not burden you with such a life, Sweet Ann."

They walked slowly and Ann thought of the great hardships the men had suffered. She'd always known of the physical dangers but now she thought of the mental anguish the partisans must have suffered.

The news of the proposal did not, as Jamie had predicted, come as any surprise, but was met with great enthusiasm. Nell Bixby was pleased for her daughter but distraught at the great distance between the two plantations. Ann's life would be far from the Bixby farm and that caused some discomfort to her loving relatives. And Jamie's plans for the wedding were a surprise.

"May, Jamie? So soon?" a distraught Nell Bixby cried. "How can we possibly lose her so soon? She is so young..."

"Now, Nell," Tom Bixby tried to comfort his wife. "Jamie is right. There is much to be done at his plantation and he needs Ann by his side. Ann is young, but this war has aged us all. There is little need to wait."

"But we have to find material for a dress. We have no black or gray,." Rachel complained.

Jamie interrupted. "This is a new day and it is time to change. I want Ann to be married in a gown of blue. Last Christmas I left a package with Ann's mother. It contains a bolt of blue silk which my mother sent for a dress for Ann."

"Dark blue?" Rachel asked.

"No. A blue like the Carolina sky, like Ann's eyes. I want my bride in a dress which will not detract from her beauty."

"Really, Jamie. What will people think?" Rachel interrupted.

"They will know that times have changed and that I choose to have my bride dressed to reflect her beautiful eyes and hair and not dressed, as convention would dictate, in grey or black."

The men nodded. It certainly seemed to them that Jamie's reasoning was valid. Times were changing and this wedding would mark a new era.

"But May? So soon?" the women argued.

"It seems a long time to me," Jamie responded. "I have the planting to see to and that should be done before the first of May. That would be a fine time for my mother and me to come for Ann."

The family finally agreed and there was only a dowry to speak of.

"No need," Jamie insisted, but Tom and Jack were determined not to be shamed by a lack of dowry.

"We can speak of it later," Jamie decided.

As the household quieted, Ann and Jamie sat near the fire talking with the two Bixby men. Excited about the young couple's nuptials, there were still questions unanswered.

Finally Tom spoke. "What about the Tories who were your neighbors, Jamie? Did they leave with the British or are they planning to stay?"

"Most gone, Tom," Jamie replied.

"The family who betrayed your father? Are they gone?"

"No," Jamie answered quietly. "Dead."

"In the skirmishes along the PeeDee and Waccamaw?"

"No. Shot from ambush. Executed, you might say."

The group was quiet. Jamie looked at Ann and answered the question he saw on her face.

"No, Ann. I did not kill them although I surely wanted them dead. But I was still in Virginia in school when the events took place. They were killed shortly after Father was hanged and before I returned."

"How, Jamie?" Jack asked.

"When my father was struggling with the men who were to execute him, mother tried to go to him and she was roughly treated. I am told that father cursed the lot and wished for them a terrible death in the face of their family."

"They were neighbors, I understand," Jack commented.

"Yes, and the hanging had little to do with politics. The McNeils wanted the plantation and had hoped in years past to join the properties by marriage. Since that wasn't going to happen, I suppose they thought that with father dead, it would be easier for the British to confiscate the property. They planned to be the ones to get it. A magistrate accompanied the Tory hanging party as well as the McNeils, father and son. Seems likely the son would get the property."

"But he didn't," Ann commented softly.

"No, Ann. He didn't. A few evenings after my father's death, Mr. McNeil was shot down in his yard, in front of his family. Shot in the head, he died instantly. When his son went to his side, he was shot. Also in the head. Few men could shoot with such accuracy at such a distance, but my father was one. It appeared to some that his ghost was taking revenge. A few days later the magistrate was shot at his dwelling. A shot to the head from the underbrush. Some tried to follow the killer but they found no trace. Tracks entered streams and ended there."

The group was silent.

Jamie continued. "The leader of the Tory militia who had been so brutal to mother and whom father had cursed, was prompted by the gossip to return to the farm to see that father was indeed dead. They dug up his grave. That was very distressing to my mother. Shortly after, he was shot from his horse and died a horrible death."

"Another shot to the head?" Tom inquired.

"Not from what I hear, and of course, I've just heard the rumors from some of the militia who joined us from time to time. Seems he was shot in the gut with a double scored shot and he died in great pain."

Ann was perplexed.

Jamie explained. "A bullet which is scored will spread on impact making a horrible wound. A single score will make the bullet dangerous but a cross cut will make it even more deadly. It also requires a great deal of caution and mastery of the weapon to make an accurate shot with such a bullet."

"Who could shoot so well?" Ann asked.

"Some who ride with Marion in the McCottry Rifles could do it," Jamie stated with little emotion. He seemed to want the conversation over.

"Could you, Jamie?" Ann asked.

"No, Ann," Jamie stated unequivocally. "Even if I had been in the state then, I probably could not have shot so well. Now that I've had lots of practice, perhaps."

"Certainly, you could now," Tom replied as he drew on his pipe. "You are a fine shot now and equal to any sharpshooter."

The group was quiet for a time. Then Ann spoke what was probably on everyone's mind.

"Ben could shoot like that, couldn't he?"

"Yes, Ann. He could."

"Have you asked him?"

"No, Ann. And I never shall. And I ask you to never ask him or my mother what they know of this business. Now I can say before God and a court of law that I did not do it and I do not know who killed my father's enemies. If I asked Ben, he would tell me the truth, and then I would know what I only suspect."

"Would anyone else suspect him?"

"No. He hunted with my father and probably became a better shot, but most slaves were not trained to such proficiency. Also, no one would suspect a slave because it would take an exceptionally fine weapon to fire such a distance with accuracy. Most would think of slaves only hunting with fowling pieces."

"But Ben has such a weapon. When Robbie Stuart tried to disarm him he was appalled that a slave would have such a weapon as Ben had."

"And I heard that you threatened to shoot him if he touched it," Jamie laughed. "What did he say when he learned that Ben belonged to me?"

"We never told him that. Uncle Jack said that Ben and the weapon belonged to General Marion and would be returned to him."

Ann hesitated, then added thoughtfully, "It would be justice if Ben shot those men with your father's gun."

"No. A sharpshooter would use his own weapon as he is familiar with that and all of us feel more comfortable with our own. The weapon Ben uses now was one my father bought for me. When I was in Virginia in school, Ben used that rifle. He still does. I use my father's rifle. Although, if he shot both McNeils, he probably used both weapons, having both loaded and ready so that after one was fired it could be slid into the sling on the saddle and the other fired when the occasion presented itself. In any case, there were no male McNeils to request our plantation and the magistrate who was in on this plot was dead, so no move was ever made on mother and her property. I'm told that people in the area still think father's ghost protects what was his, so I suspect father is avenged. But this is speculation and no one knows the truth for sure. It is best only talked about among us."

All nodded in agreement and the matter was dropped.

Twenty

Bixby Farm

Tom Bixby sat before the fire long after the rest of the household had retired for the night. Sleep did not come easy to one who hadn't slept soundly in years. In the swamp he had slept fitfully, eyes wide open with every strange sound, his hand on his weapon, ready to fight. It would be hard to adjust to safety even in his own home.

He drew on his pipe as he watched the dying fire. Occasionally the room was bathed in firelight as a flame leapt free of the coals, danced briefly, then died away.

He had only returned after years away from his family and, almost before he had time to know her again, he'd lose Ann. Five short months to know his brave daughter! His feelings were ambivalent: sad that she would leave his protection but happy for her and Jamie.

He remembered the first meeting with the young Jamie when he joined Marion. Full grown but not a seasoned warrior. He remembered Jamie's anger at his father's death and his need to actively oppose the tyranny which espoused such brutality. It did not take the young man long to become wise in the ways of warfare and comfortable in the society of swamp fighters.

Yes, he was happy for this union as he could not imagine a more suitable husband for Ann.

At a sound from behind, Tom stiffened, wary and ready for an enemy.

"Just me, Tom," Jack Bixby reassured him as he stepped into the room and moved next to the fire. "I thought all were in bed and I wanted to recheck the fire. Can't sleep?"

"Just a lot on my mind," Tom answered. "Glad that I am that Jamie and Ann are pledged, I fear I'll not have time to get to know my daughter again before she's gone."

"Aye," Jack agreed, "but it is a good match. And she'll be safe with Jamie to protect her."

"And Ben," Tom added.

"Strange conversation it was tonight. A silent killer in the swamp taking revenge. Do you have any doubt?"

"None," Tom stated emphatically. "Ben fought under my command on many occasions and he is a steady shot, with nerves of iron. He knows that rifle of his and can judge the range to a hair. And he will take a head shot whenever it's available. When we were fighting Watson at the Sampit he took out several of the gun crew. They were trying to wheel a field piece around to fire at McCottrey's Rifles which had been giving them a devastating fire. Ben had the range and he took out one man. Jamie handed him his own loaded weapon and took Ben's to reload. Ben never took his eyes off the target as he'd reach back for a loaded rifle. Other than to order Jamie to look for that devil, Watson, he spoke not another word except to mutter to his own rifle.

"Soon Watson loaded his wounded into wagons, left his dead on the field, and headed for Georgetown. He knew then that those he thought were bandits and ruffians could fight. When I complimented Ben on the fine shooting he just complained that he had not got a chance at Watson. Guess I remarked that Watson was a lucky man that he had not stepped into Ben's line of fire and Ben replied: 'Next time, Cap'n. Next time I'll kill the devil'. Our skirmishes with Watson had cost us many good men and Ben seemed to think he had to avenge them personally."

"Too bad that he never had the chance," Jack commented.

"He did have the chance at many other enemies and he killed with great efficiency and deadly calm. But we were always short of rounds. Had Ben a sufficient supply of powder and shot he would have made the enemy suffer even more."

Jack spoke quietly. "I've seen that calm. When Robbie Stuart tried to disarm him, he laid that rifle across his arm, aimed at Robbie's middle and watched him like a bird watches a snake. When Ann ordered Ezra to convey Ben to a safe place he refused to move. However, when Ann asked for his pistol he took it out of his belt and gave it to her, knowing she would not use it against him.

"When I arrived, Robbie was in a raging temper and Ann between him and Ben. She had Ben's pistol aimed at Stuart. Wanting to get that argument settled without bloodshed, I ordered Ben to leave and his only response was a gesture towards Ann. When I assured him that Ann would come to no harm, he withdrew. Yet he never turned his back on Stuart. Ben stared him down. I know that look. It conveyed stronger than words that he would shoot Robbie where he stood if Ann were harmed."

"Yes, I know he would. I'm sure he realized that Jamie had intentions toward Ann and his loyalty to the family extended to her. He would protect Ann with his life. A funny thing. Every sharpshooter names his rifle and Ben is no exception. But he rarely uses the name aloud, 'tho I've heard him call on that weapon not to let him down on occasion. He calls it Killie."

"Killie? That's appropriate for a sharpshooter. But the scored rifle shot. Was he accustomed to scoring his shots?"

Tom answered. "No, we rarely had the time and Marion would not have wanted that. But Ben meant for the man who hanged his master and abused his mistress to suffer. With a shot that spread and churned the guts, he saw to that."

"How much do you think Mrs. McCaskill suspects?" Jack asked.

"If she knows they are dead, and she certainly would, then she'd know how they died. With Ben in charge of the horses and rifles, and charged by her husband to protect her and Jamie, she would have no doubt about what had happened. But Ben is a slave. It is more than likely that Mrs. McCaskill ordered him to take such action, or at least approved of it. She's a lovely lady but, like many other ladies who have suffered greatly in this conflict, she would want revenge. Toward the last days of the fighting, as the British could no longer protect their supporters, patriot women have been the most forceful in seeking vengeance against their former tormentors."

"I suspect that even with the fighting over, there will be many killings as men reflect on the brutality meted out to their families while they were away fighting. Perhaps we should not be surprised. Certainly Rachel and Ann would shoot to kill if the need arose. And Nell, too."

"Yes, my gentle Nell would kill for me, I have no doubt," Tom decided. "But I would rather leave the killing to the men, 'tho I hope the need for violence is over. But it is time I joined my gentle Nell. Anything you want me to tend to?"

Jack shook his head.

Tom continued. "I was worried about Ann leaving our protection for times are still dangerous. There will be reprisals for months I fear, but I suspect she'll be well cared for under Jamie's protection."

He hesitated a moment, then continued "And Ben's. And Killie's"

Jamie spent the next few days with the Bixbys. He spent long hours talking with Jack about breeding horses and planting crops. He was especially interested in the kitchen gardens and what was grown there.

"It's an attractive pattern, that garden, Jack," Jamie observed.

"Yes. That is the way the Moravians lay out their plantings. We stopped in Bethabara on our way here and spent several days with them. They not only grow great crops, but they have great order in their lives which extends to their crafts and gardens. Ann has tended to this garden since she came to live with us and the plants flourish under her care."

"My mother has been able to manage the plantation since my father's death," Jamie explained, "and she understands the cash crops. We've never grown vegetables to this extent. I suspect Ann will teach me a lot about feeding my people. It was always so easy to buy what we needed from England that we never saw the need to be self sufficient. With trade closed to us, that will have to change and I look to Ann for her help. We've grown rice and greens and a few of the vegetables you have, but not the variety or the amount. "

In the evenings the family sat by the fire in the keeping room and made plans for the spring wedding. Usually the evening ended in song. Tad always wanted to sing Jamie's lassie song and Jamie obliged with gusto. He now knew that his lassie would go with him across the PeeDee and he often entertained the family by substituting words. When he sang: *Will you go, Annie, go?* Tad held his sides and laughed. Ann blushed.

With Jamie gone, the farm returned to the routine dictated by the season.

Ann spent much time working on her needlework, and helped with carding and spinning wool. Each task seemed to make the days go faster.

Ann's mother, Nell, spent much of her time preparing clothes for Ann. Although Jamie had dictated a plain wedding dress, Nell thought some decorative stitching would not be amiss. She spent long hours with her needle, working delicate stitching into the beautiful blue material.

And there were other clothes to make, also. Rachel and Nell were determined that their Ann would not arrive at the McCaskill plantation looking like a plain country lass.

Tom, Jack and Tad made plans for a large wedding. It had been decided to invite Marion's brigade, or at least those close enough to travel to the farm. That would require setting up a camp to accommodate the families and their horses. The size of the camp would depend on whether or not Marion chose to attend. If he would come, the Bixbys expected a greater crowd.

There was little word of their former guerrilla leader. Word had it that he was busy rebuilding his house and property at Pond Bluff, on the bank of the Santee. Times were hard for those who had survived the war and Francis Marion was no exception. And he was no longer a young man. He was now over fifty and the years in the swamp had surely taken their toll.

"Suppose he'll come, Tom?" Jack Bixby asked.

There was no need to ask who he meant.

"Hard to tell, Jack. He's not one for socializing but perhaps on this occasion he'll come."

Twenty-one

"General Marion will come," Tom announced as he entered the keeping room where the women were assembled. "That means that his brigade will muster in force. They'll not miss an opportunity to visit with their old commander."

Weeks before the wedding day, Jack and Tom had issued an invitation to the old brigade to muster on the farm and attend the wedding celebration. There had been many musters in the past few years which had resulted in battles and skirmishes, injuries and death. Now, with the war finally over, it was time to celebrate. What better way than a wedding?

One of the riders of the old brigade had arrived in the late afternoon with the news. He had wanted to press on before nightfall but Jack had persuaded him to stay for a meal and a night's sleep. Ann and her mother were giving last minute instructions to Hattie for the evening meal.

The days were warm but the nights were still cool and the meal would be served in the dining room. A fire would be needed to keep the chill from creeping in as darkness fell. The fireplaces would soon be cold and empty when the summer heat invaded the house.

"How many of the brigade should be expected?" Nell asked.

"Many, according to our visitor," Tom replied. "He's been following the river systems and has visited many along the Santee and PeeDee. Says there is great excitement and he expects all who can, will come."

"Then we need to make preparations soon," Nell announced. "Food and shelter must be provided if large numbers muster here."

The next days were busy with the preparations. Sites were marked off in the shade of the trees lining the bluff above the swamp. Fire pits were cleared and frames for brush arbors were constructed. Four corner posts were secured, and a roof of branches woven into a framework above. Branches with fresh green leaves would be added at the last minute to provide shade before the summer sun withered the leaves. Benches were lashed together to hold buckets for drinking water and barrels of wash water.

Since most of the men would arrive on horseback, an enclosure was erected where animals could be shaded, watered and fed. Forage for the animals had often been a problem in the days of the fighting but there would be no problem here.

The womenfolk were busy planning to feed a great number. Cured meat was taken from the storage area and hung in the smokehouse for the final smoking. Tom, Ezra and Noah would provide the fresh meat. It was hoped the hunters could find wild boar in the swamp so there would be no need to slaughter the pigs at the farm until fall. Deer came to the edge of the fields nightly so venison could be depended on. Rabbits were plentiful and Tad had a network of snares along the edge of the stream. Turtles were abundant for the rich broth which would find its way to every campfire.

Two days before the Presbyterian minister was expected

for the ceremony a jubilant Jamie rode Whiskey up to the Bixby porch and grabbed a startled Ann in an exuberant embrace.

"Jamie," a delighted but flustered Ann cried, "we didn't expect you until tomorrow. Where is your mother? And Ben? Aren't they coming?"

"Afraid not," a sober Jamie answered. "They didn't think the occasion warranted the long trip."

Ann's face fell and the sad expression prompted Jamie to cease the teasing.

"Of course, they are coming. I rode ahead and left Ben with the carriage. Mother would not miss this for the world. And she brought Maudie to attend her. They will be here within the hour. I was impatient to see you and to be sure Robbie Stuart hadn't changed your mind about marrying me."

"Oh, Jamie. How you tease! Of course I've not changed my mind."

Jamie saw the sweet smile that had occupied his dreaming for the last several months since Ann had pledged herself to him. If the truth be known, for many months before that. As he had traveled a dangerous road, thoughts of Ann and their future had given him hope in the darkest hours. But that was over now. The British were gone and the Tories were gone or were neutralized. There was no threat to this brave girl now. He thanked God daily for the peace which had come. Costly peace, but a final peace.

Jamie surveyed the surrounding fields and shaded riverbank. "Looks like Jack and Tom are expecting an army."

"General Marion is coming and all the brigade was invited so they'll want to come and renew old acquaintances. Word has come from many who will make camp here. The fire pits are ready and the cooking will start tomorrow. Papa, Ezra and Noah are planning on a big hunt to provide a large animal for every spit. Food will be plentiful."

"That will be appreciated. There were many times when we went hungry on the trail, especially after we had to join up with the Continentals. The swamp provided for us well but sometimes the pace of the campaign didn't allow for cooking over a campfire. It will be a great treat to have such bounty. Perhaps Tom can use Ben and me. We are fair shots, you know."

"I know you are and Papa will be glad for your help. Is Ben quite recovered?"

"He says he is although I think he has some discomfort occasionally. Never complains. That wound would have killed a lesser man so it's likely it twinges a bit."

"The war cost so many so much," Ann stated quietly. Although a few months had passed since the British had departed finally from Charleston, the shadow of fear and suspicion was only slowly fading from those who had suffered so much. How long would it take to obliterate the memories?

"I'd best tell Mum that your mother will arrive directly. We have her room ready but Hattie will put fresh flowers on the table and have a tea ready when our visitors arrive."

"English tea?"

"Indeed not. Hattie has many blends of herbal teas that will make you forget the bitter stuff from England," an indignant Ann informed him.

The household was ready when the carriage arrived, accompanied by Ben on his huge stallion. Jack and Rachel Bixby opened the carriage door and helped a weary and dusty Sarah McCaskill to alight.

"Welcome to our home. We hope to make your stay with us as pleasant as possible."

"Thank you. I've looked forward to this day for months and it's a pleasure meeting you and having the opportunity to meet Captain Bixby and Ann again."

Sarah McCaskill embraced Ann and then held her at arm's length. "Jamie told me you were getting more beautiful every day and I can now see that for myself."

"Thank you. This is my mother, and you know my father."

Mrs. McCaskill embraced Nell Bixby. "Such a happy occasion for both of us to unite our families through the union of these precious children. My only regret is that his father did not live to share this happiness."

From beside the carriage where she had unloaded the luggage, Maudie stood motionless but teary-eyed as she watched. Then Ann ran to her and was engulfed in a great embrace.

"Chile! Chile! How fine and pretty."

Nell Bixby came and hugged the tearful slave. "We are all indebted to you for saving Ann's life. Welcome. This day would not have happened without your courage."

Every member of the Bixby family knew of the great risk Maudie had taken in hiding Ann in a slave cabin on the McCaskill plantation. She had cured Ann of the fever, then tricked the enemy soldiers into believing that Ann was dying of the pox. Had Ann been taken as a spy she would have been hanged, if not worse. There had been many kinds of heroes in the war and Maudie was one.

"Come! Come in out of the heat," Rachel Bixby urged the assembled group into the house. Conversation was best left until Mrs. McCaskill had been refreshed and had tea.

"When do you suppose General Marion will arrive?" Sarah McCaskill asked as they sat in the parlor with their tea.

"I expect he will camp close by tonight and arrive in the early morning. He'll want to be here when the men of the brigade start arriving."

"When will that be?"

"We suggested that they come tomorrow and have tomorrow evening for visiting," Jack Bixby explained. "It will be a great muster without a campaign to plan."

"When do we hunt, Jack?" Jamie inquired.

"There will be some deer around this evening and we will take what we need, but the boars will be hunted early in the morning. You planning on joining the hunt?"

"Certainly, and Ben, too. I reckon Ben can still get a shoot between the eyes of a charging boar. Great excitement."

"This is not for sport, Jamie. The women are planning on boar on a spit by midmorning, and we dare not disappoint them. First thing you have to learn as a husband. If you want to eat well you'd best not disappoint the cooks. They've been planning for weeks. More planning than a campaign and with much happier results."

The evening hunt was not challenging as the deer came into the fields close to the house every evening. It became more of a shooting contest. The partisans' long rifles found their marks easily, the result of years of hunting game and enemies. The morning hunt would be more of a challenge and wagers were made as to who would bag the biggest boar. Jamie bet on Ben's prowess although he secretly hoped to bag the prize. It was a way of impressing his bride that he had the same skills which she so admired in her father and uncle.

The hunters entered the swamp at dawn and, soon after, shots echoed among the great trees. The sun had not been long up when the group returned with several small wild pigs and one huge boar, a victim of a proud Jamie's marksmanship. The animals had been gutted in the swamp before being secured to the mules which had been taken along to carry the game. Now, the butchering began in earnest. The small pigs were soon secured on the spits. Afraid the huge hog would not cook in time, the women felt it should be dismembered. Jack thought otherwise. Since there was plenty of food without it, he decided that the hog should be roasted whole so the assembled guests could admire Jamie's fine shooting. The women merely nodded and agreed it fitting for the groom to demonstrate he could provide food for his wife's table.

Soon the children were turning the spits and dousing the flames which flared up as the melting fat fell into the hot coals. The rich odor of roasting meat filled the air.

It was into this busy arena that General Francis Marion

rode at mid-morning. Oscar rode with him leading two sumpter mules loaded with campaign gear. Declining a room in the house, as his hosts had suspected he would, the Swamp Fox was led to the choice campsite close to the kitchen garden. From the shade of one of the great oaks, he could survey the ring of sites along the edge of the clearing. Tom and Jack offered help but little was needed. Oscar had done this many times before during the long campaign.

The rest of the morning and all afternoon riders arrived at the Bixby farm. Ezra and Noah directed the visitors to campsites and toted drinking water and wash water to each site. Most of the visitors were men but a few had brought wives and children so large kettles of stews and broths were hung at each fire pit, and breads and biscuits dispensed where desired.

Upon arrival each and every man moved to General Marion's tent to pay respects to the quiet little man who had led them in victory and defeat. Although the end of the war had seen the British leave and the revolution won, there were heartbreaking memories. These men had lost family members and comrades in the struggle. Their talk of great courage and victories was tempered with a sadness. Many fine men and loyal patriots had not lived to see this day. They were absent but they were not forgotten.

Twenty-two

The Wedding

The evening meal was festive. General Marion, at the invitation of Rachel Bixby, joined the family. Sarah McCaskill was delighted to see the partisan leader again as he had stopped at her plantation in the Waccamaw region while waging his campaign in the river systems. He had stopped to inform her of Ben's wounds and assure her of Jamie's continued health.

As had been planned, the family rose from the supper table and prepared to visit their many guests who were camped about the property. Jack had arranged for a plentiful supply of food for their supper meal. The great slabs of succulent meat would roast through the night and be ready for a wedding feast the next day.

Jack took Rachel's arm, Tom accompanied Nell. Jamie reached to take his mother's arm but she shook her head.

"General Marion, may I have the pleasure of your company?"

The little man stepped forward and offered his arm. As the two moved out to the porch, Oscar fell in behind his master. Jamie nodded to Ben who stood silently at the edge of the porch and Ben, too, moved to accompany Oscar.

Jamie reached for Ann's hand and pulled her arm through his.

"Jamie, are you expecting any trouble?"

"No, Ann. Why do you ask?"

"Oscar and Ben are armed. Does that not suggest a concern?"

"Jack, Tom and I discussed the matter and thought it wise. There will be no danger from the men of the brigade who muster here but you have neighbors in the area who were Tory and who still may harbor strong feelings against the Swamp Fox."

Ann sighed. "The war is over now. I thought we could forget about old animosities."

"Hate has a long memory, Ann," Jamie replied. "It is just well to be cautious. And 'tho your neighbors might not be comfortable with armed slaves, the men here will think nothing of it. They fought with Oscar and Ben and they know them."

As the couples moved from campfire to campfire, there was much conversation. Men thanked the ladies for the fine food and the rum. The rum was of fine quality but Jack had dispensed it sparingly since General Marion did not approve of strong drink. His preference was still a mixture of vinegar and water which he believed had kept him healthy during the long campaign.

It was a festive crowd, these reunited fighters. They greeted old comrades, exchanged stories, renewed friendships, and paid their respects to the Bixbys. A few of the old-timers remembered Jack Bixby from his days in the 2nd South Carolina Regiment before the fall of Charleston. All, of course, had fought with Captain Tom Bixby in the brigade.

Although only a few of these men had been at Snow Island when Ann had arrived to warn Francis Marion of the planned pincer attack two years before, all had heard the tale of her ride through the swamp. Those who had seen her then would scarce recognize this lovely young lady now. She had been very small and young then. Now she was taller but still slender and graceful as she walked on Jamie's arm.

Jamie introduced his bride to the guests as they moved from campfire to campfire. The young couple were the recipients of good wishes and a fair amount of teasing.

As the evening wore on the stories became more and more colorful as men reminisced about the campaigns. There had been time to mourn the losses. Now they remembered the gains. Tale after tale of bravery, daring, and just plain cussedness was told.

They talked of the raid on the British column accompanying the American prisoners from the big battle at Camden, and the terrible days in the Great Swamp where they hid from the devastation along the Santee.

Then they reminisced about the more successful raids at the Blue Savannah, Black Mingo, Tearcoat Swamp, Halfway Swamp, and Georgetown. They remembered their camp at Snow Island and the attempt by Col. Watson to trap them there. Ann's ride through the swamp to warn Marion's Brigade had allowed Marion to outsmart the enemy as they engaged them at Wiboo Swamp, Mount Hope Swamp and the lower bridge of the Black River.

And what pride in the marksmanship of McCottry's Rifles at Sampit Bridge, Fort Watson and Fort Motte!

Of Quinby Bridge they talked in hushed tones. The thought of the many good men lost there still haunted the survivors of that bloody disaster and the bitterness would remain. The end of the war brought a measure of peace, but memories were long and bitter.

The battles of the last year were rarely mentioned. The old-timers remembered the time when they fought under Marion's command with no higher command. The Continental Army had caught up with them, and they ended the war in concert with General Greene, but it was the old days they remembered here.

189

Ann thought of the pride of these men as they related the events of the campaign. They had followed a quiet little man in a guerrilla war against an invading British army and thousands of their Tory supporters.

They had persisted against great odds: Little ammunition, little pay, poor rations and miserable living and fighting conditions.

They had been hunted like animals by their enemies but they had stayed the course.

They had cut the supply lines, harassed their enemies, humbled the Tories, and had kept hope alive when there was no Continental Army in the state.

They had risked all. Some had lost all. Some had wounds that were visible. Others had invisible scars they would carry to the grave.

At a time when others had changed allegiance, some had run in the face of the enemy, these men had stood firm.

Ann thought of the unspeakable dangers, the perilous conditions, the constant threats and knew that these men would do it again, if their country needed them. Yes, if ever their country needed them, they would again follow the Swamp Fox against any enemy. Such was the dedication to liberty and the devotion to their leader, Francis Marion.

They were a motley bunch but the nation owed much to them. Without them, there would be no celebration here tonight.

And it was a great celebration. Tad had commented that it was a greater time than the fairs that used to be held in Camden. There was music, ballads being sung to simple accompaniments, a magician entertaining children, and the fiddlers and pipers were tuning up.

"Jamie! Ann!" came shouts from a barn among the outbuildings, where the threshing floor had been swept clean for dancing. "Come quick! Come dance!"

Jamie took Ann's hand and together they raced across the open fields toward the sound of the fiddlers. At the edge of the platform Jamie grasped Ann around the waist and swung her up to the dancing floor. When he had jumped up to join her, he put his arm around her as they were pushed toward the head of the line.

"This is for you and Ann, Jamie," the group informed him. "We're dancing 'Come Haste to the Wedding.'"

When Jamie gave Ann a tight hug, she blushed and he released her. She moved away from him to the head of the women's line and turned to face him.

How beautiful she is, Jamie thought. The dampness had curled her fiery hair into tight ringlets around her flushed face. The curls bounced as she nodded her head to the music. She was dressed simply in a gathered chemise and full skirt, but she could not have been more lovely if she had been gowned in satins and decorated with jewels.

Jamie bowed low to his partner and Ann bobbed a quick curtsey to him and the dancing started. Ann bowed to other dancers, turned and returned again and again to Jamie's outstretched hand. If he held her hand a little longer and a little tighter than usual, the other dancers merrily clapped the meter until the partners continued.

Each dance seemed more spirited than the previous one until the fiddlers were playing fast jigs. Finally, a perspiring Jamie shouted, "Enough." He grabbed Ann's hand, pulled her away from the dancing and lifted her down from the threshing floor. He did not release her but held her, feet swinging above the ground, until he had kissed her to the hoots and hollering of the crowd. Then, he placed her gently on her feet and hand-in-hand the two walked away.

"Jamie, whatever possessed you," Ann sputtered.

A laughing Jamie just squeezed her hand and walked on.

It was late when the socializing ceased and the Bixbys and their guest returned to the house.

"Were all those stories true?" Ann asked Jamie as they walked across the field.

"Most were. At least, in part," he replied.

"Did Ben really lift a horse?"

"Well, he didn't lift it but came close. He did save that man's life although it was a bit different than told tonight. The man was pinned under his dying horse and we were moving out when Ben saw the problem, and returned. He rolled the horse over and pulled the partisan out of the mud, sputtering and cursing like you never heard. His face had been shoved down in the muck and he was lucky to be alive. The soft muck kept him from breaking bones but he was one angry man. Ben pulled him up onto his own horse and got them both out of there with the Tories is close pursuit. The bullets whizzed close but Ben outrode the pursuers and both were safe. Had the fella been left behind he would surely have been killed."

Ann shuddered. "There were many heroes in the brigade, weren't there?"

"Not heroes, Ann. Any honorable man will exceed his limitations when what he holds dear is threatened."

The two walked on in silence. When they reached the porch the women of the household were preparing to retire. Jamie would have liked to stay and to talk. He was reluctant to let Ann go but it had been a long day and tomorrow would hold great excitement. He kissed his mother's cheek, then turned to Ann and kissed her gently.

"Good night, Ann Bixby. And this is the last time I shall address you so. Tomorrow you will be a McCaskill, but still my Sweet Ann."

Reluctantly, he walked away, then moved toward the campfires again. He had other tales to hear and tell.

The day dawned sunny and warm. The women fretted about the heat. The wedding should be as early as possible to avoid the rising temperature. They were relieved when the Presbyterian preacher arrived at mid-morning.

Neighbors had arrived and mingled with the brigade.

There seemed to be little problem. Rachel sent the message throughout the farm that the wedding ceremony would take place within the hour.

By the appointed time the area around the porch where the wedding would take place was crowded.

Jamie stood waiting. Since his father's death he was the head of the McCaskill family and he wore the tartan of the McLeod clan of Lewes Island, Scotland, the ancestral home of the clan. His tartar contained the blue of the sky, the green of the hills, and the yellow of the sun. He wore his clan's regalia with great pride. This day would start a new family, a new generation, a new day in this new country.

Finally, an impatient Jamie heard the bagpipes and the piper moved to the side of the porch. The marshall moved onto the porch and down the steps, his baton keeping the tempo. Behind him, Ann Bixby exited the house on the arm of her father.

Jamie smiled as a kinsman walked carefully backward, facing Ann. Although they expected no rival clansman to steal his bride, it was a tradition that went back to the days of the great warrior clans.

A great hush fell over the assembled guests. Jamie felt that the crowd was struck dumb by his bride's beauty, but it might have been the fact that this bride was not what was expected. Not attired in grey or black as was the custom, she wore a simple gown of sky-blue. No hoops or bustles. Just a gown of exquisite simplicity. Her red hair was pulled up into a tiny mob cap of white lace, trimmed with Carolina roses. Tendrils of red curls fell from the floral crown.

Across her breast, from shoulder to hip was a band of tartan, signifying a McCaskill bride. Jamie stepped forward as she approached and took her hand from her father.

The ceremony was short and traditional. Jamie gave his vows in a strong voice. Ann's pledge was soft but sure. When they had been pronounced man and wife the quiet was broken with a great shout.

"For Jamie and Ann;
Hip! Hip! Huzza!
Hip! Hip! Huzza!
Hip! Hip! Huzza!"

The joyous shout rang out over the assembled guests as the brigade cheered the bridal couple. There had been troubled years behind but now, with this occasion, a new era emerged.

Jamie leaned to Ann and whispered. "You're mine now, Sweet Ann. Ann McCaskill."

He took her hand and pulled it through his arm and together Mr. and Mrs. James Duncan McCaskill turned and faced their friends and their future.

And the cheering continued: Hip! Hip! Huzza!

Sources

Bass, Robert. *Swamp Fox: The Life and Times of Francis Marion.* Orangeburg, SC: Sandlapper Publishing Co., Inc., 1974.

Bynum, Flora Ann L. *Old World Gardens in the New World; The Gardens of the Moravian Settlement of Bethabara in North Carolina, 1753-72.* Washington, DC: Taylor & Francis, 1996.

James, William Dobein. *A Sketch of the Life of Brig. Gen. Francis Marion and a History of His Brigade.* Charleston, SC: Gould and Riley, 1821.

Lambert, Robert Stansbury. *South Carolina Loyalists in the American Revolution.* Columbia, SC: The University of South Carolina Press. 1987.

Lumpkin, Henry. *From Savannah to Yorktown: The American Revolution in the South.* New York: Paragon House, 1981.

Morrill, Dan E. *Southern Campaigns of the American Revolution.* Baltimore, Maryland: The Nautical & Aviation Publishing Company of America.

Moss, Kay K. *Southern Folk Medicine: 1750-1820.* Columbia, SC: The University of South Carolina Press, 1999.

Pancake, John S. *This Destructive War: The British Campaign in the Carolinas, 1780-1782.* Tuscaloosa, Alabama: The University of Alabama Press, 1985.

Rankin, Hugh. *Francis Marion: The Swamp Fox.* New York: Thomas Y. Crowell Company, 1973.

Scheer, George F., and Hugh F. Rankin. *Rebels and Redcoats: The American Revolution Through the Eyes of Those Who Fought and Lived It.* New York: A Da Capo Paperback, 1957.

Symonds, Craig L. *A Battlefield Atlas of the American Revolution.* Baltimore, Maryland: The Nautical and Aviation Publishing Company of America, 1986.

Taylor, Dale. *The Writer's Guide to Everyday Life in Colonial America from 1607-1783.* Cincinnati, Ohio: Writer's Digest Books, 1997.

Weems, M. L. *The Life of General Francis Marion: A Celebrated Partisan Officer in the Revolutionary War.* Philadelphia, PA: J. B. Lippincott Company, 1891. (Copyright, 1824. Based on a manuscript by Brig. Gen. Peter Horry of Marion's Brigade.)